THE GAY-LEN MEMOIR: HOW LOVE CAN MAKE YOU STUPID

Galen J. Cromartie

ISBN: 1976309026
ISBN-13: 9781976309021

This book is dedicated to my loving husband, my family, and anyone who has been in an abusive relationship. I chose the title *The Gay-Len Memoir: How Love Can Make You Stupid* because everyone, at least once in his or her life, has been, for lack of a better word, stupid for love. It could be something as simple as staying with a person whom you have nothing in common with, or it could be as serious as staying with someone who is abusive. Maybe you were cheated on or given an STD, or, like me, you stayed with a person who took away your choice of whom you gave your first time to. No matter the reason, love has a way of impairing our better judgment, and this is the story of how it impaired mine.

CONTENTS

PREFACE

"Nobody loves me. Maybe I should just kill myself so I don't have to go through this anymore." Thoughts of suicide crossed my mind a lot when I was a child. Love has a way of making you think and feel things about yourself that go beyond the sense of reason. "Maybe I should just take the easy way out so I won't have to go through the struggles of finding love. Why even bother to be in love? Seems like nothing comes from it but hurt and pain. I deserved this. I did something to make him mad," I kept telling myself. "That's the only explanation for his hitting me even though he says he loves me." Looking back, I see that all of my relationships were filled with nothing but hurt and pain. I can't blame everything on my exes. I could've left them at the first sign of bad behavior, but I stuck around. What does that say about me? I always tell my friends not to put up with things they shouldn't have to deal with in relationships, like abuse and cheating, but I can't take my own advice. When it comes to relationships, it's easier to give advice than to take it.

I think I picked up a lot of what love meant to me from my childhood. I watched my mom stick around and be so caring and loving toward men who treated her so badly, ones who didn't appreciate how strong she was. As I was growing up, my mom was definitely my hero, but I didn't realize that seeing the things she went through would have such an effect on the type of men that I would end up dating. I dated some men who were identical to the ones who treated my mother so wrong, even though I knew that this wasn't how love should be. Seeing it as a child almost gave me the impression that this was what real love looked like, and if a man wasn't cheating, lying, or putting his hands on me, then it wasn't normal. So, I grew to expect that type of treatment from men as the normal thing. I expected that the one thing I could always count on in a relationship was getting hurt.

Sometimes I wish being gay were actually a choice so I could just date women. People love to say that being gay is a choice, but I'm not sure what sane person would choose to go through life being hated by people who have different views of what a "normal" relationship is—not to mention having to fight for basic rights like marriage, health insurance, and even something as simple as safety.

My experiences with love have included being beaten till I didn't think I was going to survive, being cheated on so many times I felt like I was worthless, and being raped by someone I thought I loved. Seemed like hurt and pain were all I knew from love, but all of that changed the day I met the man who is now my loving husband. He loved me through all of the pain and hurt I went through with all of my exes. For the first time in my life, I'm not worrying about a man cheating on me or lying and hiding things. I don't fear for my safety. I know this man will never raise a hand to me, and that's something I never knew could feel so good. I needed a chance to tell my story, to tell others about the struggle and pain I went through on my journey to find real love. Throughout this process, I learned how strong I was and also how worthless I had viewed myself to be. I learned that it is OK to be alone and that you don't need anyone to validate your happiness. As hard as it was for me to accept this over the years, I finally learned what having self-worth and self-love means. I hope that this book helps give strength not only to those who are in a bad situation and don't have the strength to get out but also to those who have gone through things and haven't talked about it.

ACKNOWLEDGMENTS

Thanks to all of my family who helped me through all of my breakups, who helped me not only move on with my life but move out of apartments when my boyfriends refused to do so. Thanks to my mother for being my rock, my cousins for being my muscle, my friends for being my brain. I love all of you very much, and I wouldn't be able to do this without you. Thanks to my friends who gave me advice that sometimes I ignored because I was hardheaded, although I knew they had my best interest at heart. Most importantly, thank you to all of the horrible-ass men I dated who gave me the material I needed to write this book.

1

THE BEGINNING AND END OF AN INNOCENT CHILD

Growing up gay in a small town in South Carolina in the nineties was extremely difficult. Anderson was located in the Bible Belt, and being gay then wasn't as glamorous as being gay in a major city today. As far back as I can remember, I've always had an attraction for men. My first experience with being attracted to the same sex was in the third grade. My childhood best friend was someone whom I had this attraction to, but being a kid, I didn't know what it meant to be gay. I mean, what normal third grader is thinking about an attraction to anyone, especially someone of the same sex? I didn't know what it was about Frankie, but I was infatuated with him for some reason. To this day I'm not completely sure why I was so attracted to him. It probably could've been anyone who piqued my interest, but because we hung out all the time, it just happened to be him.

There's a huge misconception that something happens to children when they're young that makes them gay—like some type of molestation. I've been asked a lot if someone in my family molested me or taught me how to be gay, as if it were something that could be taught. It also seems like people think that gay men tend to be child molesters, which is ridiculous and probably one of the most offense stereotypes that's out there. A real close friend of mine actually told me she wouldn't let one of her gay friends around her children because she felt that he would try to molest them. Obviously, our friendship deteriorated after that. I can assure you that I was never molested. I would like to think I was born this way.

As a child, I always saw myself marrying the man of my dreams, being with someone who would show me unconditional love and affection. I didn't really know a lot of other gay people when I was a kid. It wasn't something you saw on TV a lot in the 1990s, and it wasn't talked about. The only way I could express myself was when Frankie came over; we would play house, and I would always end up playing the female. I'm not saying that I wanted to be a female, but with him I wanted to feel like he was in some kind of control.

What do you do when you're a child and you're attracted to the same sex? Do you go to your parents, or in my case, my mom, and say, "Hey, Mom, I'm gay"?

There was a time when I wanted to talk to my mother about it, but how would I even begin to have that conversation? My mother is one of the most loving people in the world, but even when you're very young, there is always the fear of being disowned if you tell your family that you're gay.

The hardest part of my young gay years was trying to establish my identity as not only a gay man but a black gay man. There were no men like me on TV. Most shows had a stereotypical version of what they thought a gay man was. It seemed we were reduced to nothing more than slim, flamboyant bitches. I didn't feel like I fit that mold; I wasn't the most masculine child, but I also wasn't overly flamboyant.

I really came into my sexuality in middle school, when I started to notice there were more guys out there like me that I could relate to. This is also when I noticed there were different types of gay. I noticed some guys dressed a lot more femininely than I did, or they spoke with a more feminine voice. This is also when I started to learn that gay men could be petty as hell. Middle school was full of cute guys, and even though I didn't know fully what these gay feelings were, I knew I wanted to explore that side of me. My first crush was on this cute white guy in my class. I think he was gay too, but he wasn't as open about his feelings as I was. We would pass each other in the hall and give each other looks and smiles. He was the cutest guy I had ever seen. I finally got up enough courage to talk to him, and he was nice and didn't blow me off. The more we talked, the more we wanted to hang out and be around each other. We would meet in the bathroom and kiss, and we would also send little notes to each other in class. He was a lot more aggressive about the things he wanted to do in the bathroom, which led me to believe that he had a lot more experience doing things with guys than I did. He may not have been open about his feelings at first, but as time went on, he started to be a lot more verbal. I looked forward to meeting him in the bathrooms daily—that is, until we were caught. I'm not even sure how the teacher knew what we were doing in the bathroom. He didn't come in, he just opened the bathroom door and said, "OK, guys, come out of the bathroom." I was so afraid he was going to call my mother and tell her what we were doing. Luckily, he just sent us both back to class. After that, my guy decided to not talk to me anymore. I was saddened by it, but life moved on. Guess that was my first experience with disappointment when it came to men.

After that incident, I really wasn't comfortable talking to guys again until I got to high school; that was where my hormones really started to grow. Since I knew that I was going to start dating soon, I decided it was time to come out to my mother. It was the early 2000s, and homosexuality was starting to become more mainstream in the media, so this made it a little easier for me to start the conversation. That was one of the hardest things I've ever had to do. I was sixteen at the time, and I got a lot of advice from my friends about how I should approach the situation. Again, I knew my mom wouldn't disown me, but I had heard about so many stories of families kicking their kids out just because they were gay. It wasn't even my mom that I was worried about but my stepdad. We seemed to fight a lot, and I didn't know how he would react to the news when she told him.

I actually didn't say the words that I was "gay"; instead I decided to make my mom guess. I had her come in my room and said, "Mom, I have something to tell you," but I didn't want to say the words, so I made her guess. Eventually she asked if I was gay, and I nodded and said yes. She looked at me and smiled and said she loved me just the same, and it didn't matter that I was gay. I couldn't have been happier with what she said. When you're a child, the biggest fear you have is somehow losing the love of your parents or disappointing them. At that moment I was relieved, and I cried because I just hadn't known how that conversation would go; I was just so glad that it went in a positive way. For the first time, I felt like I could truly be myself and not hide who I was. The freedom you get from coming out is truly amazing, as you no longer have to pretend to be something you aren't.

Those four years of high school were some of the best and most traumatic years of my life. I had good friends, and I was able to be out with people, but unfortunately I didn't have a boyfriend. I did flirt with a few guys I had class with, but nothing serious. That was until I met Andre, and everything changed. He was so sexy, tall, dark, and juicy all over. He had a deep, sexy voice that would make any man melt. One day at school, he walked up to me in the cafeteria and just started a conversation with me. He had been eyeing me walking around school and always wanted to come up and talk to me, but I was always with my friends. He had just decided to stop waiting for me to be alone and approach me. He thought I was cute, and I thought he was sexy, so without hesitation we decided to exchange numbers. I didn't have a cell phone yet, but I gave him the number to my grandma's. We talked on the phone a lot, and we spent a lot of time together while at school. He was blatant with his sexual attraction toward me; he would get his dick hard in class and tell me to look over at it. I thought this was cute. I'd never had a guy be so bold with me, and it made me feel special. At the same time, I was wondering what the hell I was going to do with that thing. I hadn't seen a lot of dicks, but that thing was huge—the biggest that I've ever seen. Sex wasn't something I thought about other than pleasuring myself. I didn't want to gain a reputation around high school like some of the other gay guys I knew.

Andre and I would hang out every day after school, and he didn't seem to mind that people started to notice us being all up under each other. One day I missed the bus, and he decided to walk with me to my house. When we got there, he asked me if I wanted to make it exclusive. I couldn't believe my ears. He would be my first real boyfriend. I immediately said yes and asked, "What the hell took you so long to ask?"

I really liked him, and he was telling me he loved me on a daily basis. After we had been dating for about a month, Andre asked me if I wanted to come see him later at his house. We'd never hung out at each other's houses before, so I was looking forward to spending some alone time with him. I couldn't wait to leave school so I could go by his house. I told him to give me a call when he was ready, and right when I walked in the door from school, he called. "Come over to my house. I want to see you," Andre said.

"OK, I'll be right over," I replied. Luckily, we didn't live far away from each other, so I walked over to his house.

When I got there, he said, "You looking good, baby. Get your ass over here and give me a hug." I loved the way he would talk to me.

His parents weren't home at the time, so we had the whole place to ourselves. I was there for maybe five minutes before he said, "Do you want to fool around?"

I was scared since I'd never done anything with a guy before, but he was my boyfriend, so I figured I would do maybe some oral sex at least.

"We have to go out back though since my parents might be home soon."

That statement made zero sense to me. His parents were already out of the house, so why would we need to go outside to do anything? I was naïve, and I was getting a little nervous, as I'd never done anything like that before, but again I obliged. We went out back, and he told me to get on my knees and give him some head. I was happy to do it, but that was all I was going to do. This wasn't how I had thought it would be the first time he and I took it to that level. I was outside and very uncomfortable. The way he said, "Get down on your knees," was not loving but demanding. As sexy as verbal commands can be at times, this wasn't the time for that since it was our first time. It made me feel a little apprehensive toward him.

"I'm not comfortable doing all of this outside," I said to him, but he didn't seem to care.

"Let me get some ass then," he said, as if that were somehow better than my sucking his dick.

"No," I replied. "I'm not ready for that, nor do I want to do it outside."

"Please, baby, let me just stick the tip in. You love me, don't you? Then you will let me do it."

I'm not sure how that saying got started or why it almost always seems to work on people, but it worked on me. I'll be honest: I was afraid to even let his dick anywhere near my ass. It was the biggest dick I've ever seen. It had to be at least twelve inches long and was crazy thick. If I had to compare it to something, I would say it was the size of an air freshener can. Finally, I gave in. "OK, but just for a second, and you cannot put all of that in me." He agreed, and I turned around and pulled down my pants. "You don't have any condoms or lube with you?" I asked.

"No, but we don't need them," he said.

The moment he tried to put it in, I was in pain. There is no real way to prepare for the pain that comes with your first time; the only thing someone can do is try to be gentle, but this was not the approach Andre decided to take. I turned to try and end it, and he grabbed me and pushed his dick inside me. I yelled out in pain and said, "What the hell are you doing?"

Again, he used the line, "If you love me, you will let me finish."

"Stop! You are hurting me. Why are you doing this?" The pain was indescribable. I started to cry as seconds turned into minutes, and minutes felt like an eternity. I tried to pull away, and he pulled me back to him. I could do nothing but cry. How was he able to do this to me while I was screaming in pain? There was no way to prepare my mind or my body for this, and no matter how much I yelled, he wouldn't stop. I knew nobody would come to help me. I'm not sure how I would even have felt if someone had walked up and seen this happening to me. He finally let out this scream. He was finished, and I could feel his nut running through me. I was finally able to run away from him. I wiped my eyes and pulled up my pants, but before I could get my underwear on, I noticed blood and nut running down my legs. I couldn't believe he had come inside of me, and to make things worse, I had to walk home with this dripping between my legs.

He looked at me and said, "I love you," but all I could do was just look at him; I was still crying and feeling disgusted. "Don't tell anybody this happened. If you do, I'll just deny it. Who will believe you anyway?" I didn't say anything to him.

The walk back to my grandma's house felt like it took so much longer than the walk to Andre's had. The faster I walked, the more fluid seemed to leak from my body. I felt so nasty; I couldn't believe this had just happened to me. Finally, I got to my grandma's, and, as clichéd as it sounds, the first thing I did was take a shower. It was the longest shower I'd ever taken. I cried and cried and cried until my eyes were bloody red.

Whom could I tell this to? Who would even believe me? I hadn't come out to anyone in my family except for my mother, and there was no way I could tell her about this. If I told my cousins, I'd first have to admit that I was gay and then also admit that I had been raped. I decided to say nothing to anyone. What a lonely feeling and a heavy burden to carry. Even as I write this, neither my mother nor anyone else in my family knows that this happened to me.

The saying that you will always remember your first is true, but for me, what should've been passion and intimacy was aggression and anger. Passing Andre in the school halls was so uncomfortable; he would walk past me and pretend I didn't exist. I thought sex, even if it was forced, was supposed to bring a couple together, not drive them apart. I don't think he could face me. One day I'd had enough of him ignoring me, so I decided to confront him. "How could you do that to me and then just ignore me?" I asked.

"I don't know what you are talking about," he responded.

When he said that, it felt like I got hit in the head with a sledgehammer. He was just going to pretend that nothing had happened and that he hadn't taken away my right to choose whom I had my first time with. He just gave me a mean look and walked away from me. I'd never felt so low. Even though he walked away from me, he couldn't avoid me forever since we had a class together. Even in class, however, I was invisible to him. He never looked at me, and he never talked to me. I tried several times to go up to him and have a conversation—not because I missed him but because I needed some answers. I guess eventually he was tired of avoiding me and walked up to me, asking if we could talk.

"It's over," he said. "I don't have feelings for you. I got what I wanted from you, and now we're through. Don't try to talk to me anymore, and don't try to tell anyone what happened. I assure you, nobody will believe you."

I froze. I was speechless at how cold he could be. "Fine. You never have to worry about my even looking in your direction ever again," I said as I walked away crying.

I couldn't talk to anyone about what had really happened, so I had to just cry to my friends, saying I had just been dumped. If this was what love was, I knew I didn't want to have anything else to do with it. I decided to swear off men for a very long time and just focus on getting out of high school. Of course, that really didn't last long because I was going through puberty, and all I could think about was guys. I did at least take some time to heal from the breakup, but I don't think I could ever heal from the rape, and sex for me would never be the same.

2

IF YOU LOVE ME, THEN WHO IS SHE?

I needed something to occupy my time, so I decided to get a job—my first job—at the local Hardee's in Anderson. One day while I was working my shift, one of my then friends mentioned how he had this homeboy named Eric he thought I would be perfect for. I was still apprehensive about getting back out there after my last fiasco relationship, but I wanted to move forward, so I agreed to meet him. When Eric walked through the doors of the restaurant, my jaw hit the floor. In walked this light-skinned, sexy, thick, brown-eyed dude with this fat ass. He walked up to me and introduced himself, and I tried, but failed, to remain calm. I wasn't the most experienced person in the ways of being flirted with, so I couldn't do anything but smile and giggle. I gave him my number, as he stated he didn't have a direct phone of his own for me to call.

Later that night, I met up with him in a nearby parking lot. I hadn't expected him to reach out to me so soon, but I was happy that he had. We talked for a while, and his game was out of this world, right up to the point he told me he was on the down low. Of course, I had no idea what this meant at the time, but I didn't care. He exuded this confidence, which was such a turn-on, it didn't matter what he was telling me. Eric—who was a few years older, mind you—was complimenting how my ass fit in my jeans, how my lips were looking soft and kissable. In fact, after the first thirty minutes of talking, we were kissing in his car. When Andre paid me compliments, they had been more blunt and abrasive, but when Eric gave me a compliment, it was genuine and sweet. When we left each other, I was feeling high as a kite, floating on a cloud of possibilities about the happiness that was ahead of me, or so I thought.

Days turned into months, and our relationship grew stronger. Being that Eric was on the down low I did not have his phone number, so every day I had to wait by the phone for him to call me. At first this was fine, but as time grew, I needed more than he was giving me, and then the drama started.

My birthday was around the corner, and he promised to take me out to the club to celebrate. Funny thing about that was, he had no damn car. We went to the happening club at the time, Spooneys, and I was having the time of my life with my "boyfriend," until he decided he didn't want to dance with me anymore; he wanted to dance with the attractive guy he'd been staring at the whole time. The more he danced with that bitch, the angrier I got over the utter disrespect he was showing me on the most important day of my life. Right as I went to confront him, one of our mutual friends got into a fight and had to be taken to the emergency room. Of course, since I was the only person driving, we had to take my car, but Eric took my keys and was about to leave me at the club while he pulled out in my car. This was yet another strike against him. How are you going to drive off in my car and leave me on my birthday? I had to run out of the club to my car to catch up to him. We argued all the way to the hospital and continued to argue when we got there. We spent what felt like an eternity waiting on our friend to get her stiches done. Finally, she was finished, and we could leave. Eric and I, along with several of our friends, went back to his house to spend the night. There was just one problem with that: I wasn't allowed to stay. Not because anyone there wasn't aware that we were dating but because his ho ass wanted to have sex with one of my friends, and he knew that wouldn't happen if I was there. I grabbed my stuff and left, but being the fool I am, I swept it under the rug because I was in love.

When I got back home, I tried calling the number I had for him, but he never answered my calls. I stayed up all night thinking about what they were more than likely doing behind my back.

He must've felt some way about his actions, because he tried to make it up to me the following night by inviting me over for a romantic dinner. I got to his place, and it appeared there was only one thing on his mind. "Did you fuck him?" I asked.

"Of course I didn't," he said. "Why would I do that knowing that we are together?"

I couldn't believe he was trying to get some after the stunt he had pulled. I was nervous to give him any because the first time I'd had sex was one of the worst experiences of my life. I didn't want to tell him what had happened to me, and I knew I couldn't make him pay for what my ex had done to me either. He really didn't deserve anything from me, especially considering how he had been acting, but when he pulled his dick out, that changed everything. Not to sound like a size queen, but it wasn't the biggest dick I've ever seen, not to mention my first encounter with dick had been with someone who was insanely endowed. He looked at me and said, "I know it isn't that big, but maybe we can bring someone else in to fuck you while I suck your dick." If looks could kill, that room would've looked like something out of a Wes Craven movie. The way he said it made it seem like it was something he had been thinking about for a while.

I put my fears to the side and decided to have sex with him. He was my boyfriend, after all, and he sensed that I was nervous, so he did everything he could to make me feel comfortable. However, the sex wasn't good at all, and I literally felt nothing. I couldn't tell when he started or when he finished, and I had this look of dissatisfaction on my face that even Ray Charles could see. I'll give him one thing though: he could suck a mean dick.

For a long time, Eric kept pressuring me to have a threesome with one of his friends whom I had never met. No matter how many times or ways he asked me to do that, my answer was always no. I asked him if he was interested in meeting some of my friends, but with him being down low, he said that I couldn't tell them that we were dating, and he would only come if I referred to him as just a friend of mine. I don't lie to my friends, so I told them what was really going on, but they had to pretend like they didn't know. I invited him over to meet them, which ended up being a big mistake. When he came in, he was acting extremely cold toward me. He certainly didn't act like a friend of mine, and later on I found out that he'd told my friends that the only reason he was around me was for a ride and some money. After they told me that, I went straight to Eric and cussed him out. What kind of boyfriend says that about someone he claims to love? It did make me think, however; he had come to get my car several times on a Saturday night to go out to the club. Not once did he ask me to come with him; he just came to get my car and left. I was a teenager, and it was my first car, so I was terrified that my mother would wake up and realize my car was gone but I was still there. A few times he didn't bring it back until hours after he had claimed he would.

He still wouldn't leave the threesome idea alone. He actually suggested it be with my best friend, whom he'd met. Funny, Eric didn't want my friend to know he was gay, but now suddenly he wanted me to try to convince him to have sex with us. When he would run into my best friend in a public place, Eric would even be all extra and unnecessarily nice, trying to "try him." My best friend was straight, and I wouldn't even attempt to put him in that situation, but my so-called man was only interested in satisfying his own needs. I quickly shot him down when he brought the idea up, but that sure didn't stop him from trying to get with him on his own. Thank God for good friends, because all of the stuff Eric would say to my friend made its way right back to me.

He wasn't my first boyfriend, but he was the first man I ever loved to that extent, and looking back I think he set the tone for how the majority of my relationships would turn out.

One day he told me he had something he wanted to talk to me about, and he asked if I could come over. I went over, and he sat me down and said that people were starting to talk—rumors were going around that he might be gay. I told him, "Well, you are gay, so what's the big deal?"

He said, "The big deal is that I'm on the down low, and you knew that from the beginning, so to dial back the rumors, I'm going to get a girlfriend."

I looked at him and said, "Excuse the complete fuck out of me?"

He informed me that the girlfriend would only be for appearances and that he would have no feelings for the girl; it wouldn't be real. I knew that was bull when it came out of his mouth, but he had a way of manipulating me into doing almost anything for him. Of course, I wanted to know if he would be sleeping with the girl. He told me no, but he had a big-ass grin on his face, so I knew it was a lie. I couldn't even get a date with my so-called man because of his status, but I had to constantly run into him and this bitch all around town. This was my first experience having to deal with someone who was, in a sense, cheating on me. When Eric would pass by me, he wouldn't even look in my direction, which I think hurt me the most. Someone I loved, whom I did so much for, could just walk by me and act as if I were a total stranger. This took me right back to how I had felt with Andre.

One thing I hate about down-low dudes is how they are so open with the dudes they are fucking, but they never tell the female they are dating. Women are the real smart ones here because they wouldn't deal with no bull like that.

I figured if Eric could have a girlfriend on the side, why couldn't I have another boyfriend? So, when

I brought this up, he looked like he wanted to slap the pure shit out of me. How could this be though? He was able to have sex with a female, but somehow it would be different if I went and got another boyfriend. He considered it cheating if I went and did that, and he explained to me that if I chose to do it anyway, he would dump me the minute he found out about it. Since I didn't want to break up with him, I complied and stuck around with the mess of a relationship we had for a few more months. Seemed like the only thing we could do was have sex, and it wasn't even good enough to keep me satisfied. Especially knowing that his dick was being passed around to other people.

Since I knew he had a girlfriend, I thought it was only fair that we all know about each other, so I suggested that he tell her about me and we all meet and be on the same page. He said no to that of course, and I came back and said, "Either you tell her, or I will." That instantly started an argument that went nowhere. Eric never put his hands on me, but he did make me feel threatened in that moment. He wasn't the type to want anyone in his business, and he was so concerned that people were going to find out about him.

I needed some space after that conversation, and I decided we should have a short separation so I could figure out what I wanted out of life. I was young, in pretty decent shape, and attractive. I could easily find someone else who would give me the love and attention I needed.

During our break, I decided to go out on some dates with a couple of guys who weren't afraid to show me some attention out in public. I was out on a date with this real sexy dude. He had a huge football player's build, and when you saw him you wanted to straddle him. We were out at the movies, and while he was getting the tickets, I decided to go use the bathroom. When I walked out, Eric was walking in. He stopped me and asked how I was doing. I really didn't want to talk to him, especially since he was out with his girlfriend. We walked away from the bathrooms, and before I could get any further words out, he said, "Who are you here with?"

I told him that it was none of his business since he was here with his girlfriend. "Maybe you should worry about your bitch," I said.

Right when I said that, my date walked over to me and put his hand around me and said, "Hey, babe, are you OK?" He was looking Eric up and down, hoping he would say something disrespectful.

"I'm fine, baby. Do you have our tickets?"

He handed me the tickets, and I looked at Eric with a smirk as we walked off toward our theater. Regardless of whether things worked out between me and my date, having him with me in that moment made talking to him worth it.

The moment we sat down in the theater, my phone started going off. My date asked me if it was the dude from the lobby, and I had to tell him the backstory on Eric. He wasn't bothered at all, which I loved.

I ignored every call and every text until later that night. I'd never received so many phone calls from Eric while we were dating, and the moment he saw me out with someone else, suddenly I was important. In those messages he sent me, he called me every name in the book. "You fucking that nigga?" he asked. "You ain't nothing but a ho." This was followed by, "I'm sorry. I miss you so much...please call me." He was trying to get some type of reaction from me. Some of the things he had said did hurt my feelings though. How could it be OK for him to have me and a girlfriend, but when we were on a break and I went out on a date, he thought I was a ho and all the other stuff he'd called me?

I decided I wanted to talk to Eric and let him know what was on my mind. When I arrived, he tried to give me a hug, but I just moved out of the way and sat down. He asked me how I'd been and wanted to make small talk, but I wasn't having any of that. "You were out of line," I told him. I couldn't believe how much of a jerk he was being toward me. He apologized, but what came out of his mouth didn't matter to me. "I deserve better than what you are willing to give me— someone kind and someone loving. Most importantly, someone I don't have to share. It's over." I stood up to walk toward the door, and he jumped in front of me and tried to talk to me, but I was over it and over him.

I told him to get out of my way. When he did, I walked out the door and said, "Don't call me ever again." He didn't listen to me of course, but I changed my number to ensure I never had to hear his voice again. It was time for me to find someone I didn't have to share. I'd had enough of dating in high school and focused on my studies. I graduated from high school in 2004 with a 3.2 average and decided to enroll myself at ITT Technical Institute. I wasted a year and a half there but decided that school wasn't for me. I enrolled at Tri-County Technical College in spring of 2008. I decided to peruse an associate's degree in office systems technology.

3

MY STOLEN IDENTITY

I decided to give online dating a try. It isn't easy meeting my type of gay man in public. I usually go for the manly men, but they are not easy to spot in public since they appear straight. I decided to start with this website I was hearing about called Adam4Adam. That's how I met Rocky. He was the first guy I ever met online. I had never talked to someone who wasn't in my immediate area before. He lived almost four hours away from me. I am a needy person, and not being able to see someone I'm talking to often wasn't ideal for me.

I'm not really sure what drew me to Rocky at first. He wasn't the best-looking guy, but he had a hardness to him that I found attractive. He was smart too—very well spoken and educated, considering that he hadn't finished school. We had been talking for a few weeks. He was attentive and kind, and whenever he said he would call, he actually did. He seemed very trustworthy, a man who kept his word. We had talked of meeting, but he didn't drive or work, which made it hard to plan on going down to visit him; I was in school and working three jobs at the time. I overlooked the fact that he didn't have a job, car, or his own place, because I was just starting out myself, and even though I did have a job and a car, I was also still living at home. My mother always had this saying: "Whenever you are dating someone, make sure they have equal or more than what you have, or else you are already starting backward." That was advice I wish I had listened to and not ignored.

The time had finally come that I was able to go visit Rocky, and I couldn't have been more excited to meet him. I wasn't looking forward to driving almost four hours, but I really wanted to see what he was all about in person. When I got there and he came outside to give me a hug, I was shocked. He looked way better in person than he did from the photos. He lived with his mother and brothers, whom I didn't meet immediately. As soon as I got to his house, I went straight to his bedroom, and he closed the door. We talked for hours, and it was actually one of the best conversations I'd ever had with a guy.

It was understood that I would be spending the night at his house, but that dream quickly busted. He told me I wouldn't be able to spend the night because his mother wouldn't allow it. So I had to find a place to stay, but I didn't know the area at all, and I didn't know where I would go. I was so pissed because this was something we had discussed ahead of time, but when I got there, it was a different story.

These were the days before smartphones, so I had to use his computer to check my bank accounts. I didn't have the money for a hotel, so when I left Rocky's house, I ended up having to sleep in my car at a rest stop. Sleeping in my car was one of the most humiliating things I've ever had to do. He tried to call and make sure I was OK, but honestly I was so mad I didn't want to talk. Somehow, I managed to get a few hours of sleep and reached out to Rocky when I got up. He said he'd told his mother I had driven hours to stay with him, and so I was going to be spending the night the rest of my visit. When I arrived at his house, the first thing I did was take a shower. I smelled like I had slept in my car. He apologized and told me how he was ready to get his own place because his mother tended to get a little controlling at times and because he had to take care of his brothers but didn't really want to.

Before the term "superhero complex" existed, I believe I was a captain saver ho. I had this complex where I felt I had to save everyone or help people get out of bad situations. He got all in my feelings, and then he ended up getting all in me. Our first sexual encounter wasn't great since his door wouldn't lock, and we were afraid someone would come in the room. Despite the bull of not having a place to stay my first night, I actually enjoyed myself with him. He seemed like a nice guy, and he was not in the closet, which was a huge bonus for me. Not only that, he was masculine, which was big for me back then. When I left to go back home, he let me know how sad he was, and he said he wanted to come back with me. He even shed a tear, which I thought was the sweetest thing.

A few months after our first visit, our feelings for each other grew so strong we started talking about moving in with each other. That was a big step for me, leaving the comfort of my mother's home for the first time, as I was still a teenager when Rocky and I started dating. I decided to go see Rocky again so we could talk in person about the decision to move out together. This time I actually got to stay with him on the first night without incident. When I arrived, he definitely showed me how much he had missed me by putting it down. His mother and brothers were gone, and he made sure to make good use of our time. When we were finished, he looked at me and told me that he loved me. That was the first time he said it to me.

He heard his mom come back in, and he went to let her know I was there. They needed to go to the store, and she asked me if I would mind driving them there since none of them had cars. I didn't mind since she was letting me stay in her house, so I drove them to the Piggly Wiggly up the street. They went in, and I stayed in the car. After they'd been in the store about forty minutes, I got out of the car and started walking toward the store. As I was walking, I noticed a clerk from the store walking toward me. He stopped me and asked if I was with a young black man and his mother. Hesitantly I said yes, and he proceeded to tell me they were being arrested for shoplifting and there was a possibility I would be arrested as well as an accomplice. The look on my face let him know I had nothing to do with what was going on, so he took me inside the store over to where they were being held. When I saw them, especially Rocky, I wanted to pounce on him right in front of the security. The police finally arrived and escorted them off to jail. The only reason I didn't go was because I pleaded my case on how I had no idea what they were planning to do. Then I had to remember how to get back to their house to let everyone know what was going on.

While I was waiting on them to get out of jail, the anger in me was growing. All I could think about was, what if I'd been locked up? After about six hours, Rocky came through his bedroom door. I by no means condone putting your hands on someone. However, the rage took over me, and I slapped the holy piss out of him and yelled, "Are you stupid?"

The only thing he could say to me was, "I'm sorry." He blamed everything on his mother and said it had been her idea. I didn't give a frog's fat ass whose idea it was; I could've gone to jail over some bull.

I was going to leave and go back home after that, but I decided to stay; after all, I "loved" him. This was another case where love impaired my judgment. Rocky told me how he needed to get away from this environment, and he wanted us to have our own place away from the drama. When it was time for me to leave, I didn't have the same level of sadness as I had before. Probably because I was still pissed about the whole situation.

When I got home, I took some time to think about whether the relationship was something I really wanted to be in. Rocky kept apologizing to me, and he kept pointing the finger at his mother. I decided to forgive him—I guess because it's not like I got arrested, and he was being so sweet and sorry about the situation. I decided I wanted to take him up on his offer to move, and I started looking for places. I always thought my first apartment would be on my own, not living with anyone, but since he was my boyfriend and I loved him, I didn't mind very much. I looked all over, but I didn't have much money, and there is only one place in Anderson where people with limited funds stay: the Earl Homes. I got us a two-bedroom apartment, paid the deposit, and took care of all the paperwork.

The only thing left for us to do was to move in, but that also meant that Rocky had to move here, and since he had no car, that meant I had to drive down to where he was and help him move. I didn't really want to do that, but what was I going to do, not help my boyfriend move to where our new apartment was? He didn't have much stuff to move, so I went down there the very weekend I got our apartment. When I pulled up, he instantly started to put his stuff in the car. I asked him what was the rush, but before I could get the words all the way out of my mouth, his father came out and asked just what the hell he thought he was doing. I turned and asked Rocky, "What is he talking about?" Apparently my boyfriend had neglected to tell his family that he was moving out of their house and in with his boyfriend. I looked at him with this confused look, and the only question I could form was, "Are you serious? Why would you not tell your parents that you are moving?"

The next thing I knew, I was being pushed out of the house like I'd done something wrong. The father told me that if I didn't move my car out of his driveway, he would call the police on me. Rocky said he didn't care about the rest of his stuff and that he would just send for it later; all he wanted to do was get the hell out of there. Yet again, I was put in a bad situation and wasn't warned beforehand about the drama coming down the pipeline.

We finished loading what we could into my car, and I peeled out of the driveway. Of course I cussed him out yet again for putting me in another uncomfortable situation. His parents hated me now because they thought I was the crazy boyfriend who stole their son away. Who could blame them? That was the perception they had of me during the few visits I took there. It was a long drive back to Anderson after all of that, filled with a lot of awkward silence.

We arrived at the new apartment, and I couldn't wait to get in it and start our new lives together. Thankfully, Rocky liked the apartment I had picked, although since he didn't have a job to help me pay any of the bills, his opinion didn't matter much to me. The first night was great. We had sex in every room of the house, and I must say it was better than any of the other times. Guess having your own space to do it in without fear of interruption will do that.

Since Rocky didn't have a job or a car, I decided to try and find a job where we could work together that would also accommodate my school schedule. Our first joint job was at Frigidaire, and it was one of the worst jobs I ever had. There was nothing but a bunch of messy-ass females in there, and the moment they found out I was gay and had a boyfriend who also worked there, they seemed to target us. Rocky started to make friends during his time there, which was nice; I didn't want him feeling like I wanted him all to myself, even though I kind of did. Since he was working now, he could start paying for things on his own and helping with the bills.

We worked there for about three months without incident until he got laid off. "He told me that some girl claimed that he had sexually harassed her. Because he was gay, I didn't understand why they would even take the claim seriously." They also fired him without talking to him to hear his side of the story, which I found odd. I had him open a case with the Equal

Employment Opportunity Commission (EEOC) to fight it. Something just didn't add up to me. Frigidaire ended up settling with him and gave him some money to not take the ordeal further than it needed to go.

Rocky ended up getting a restocking job at Walmart, and I started to notice he came home with a lot of "damaged" electronics, like iPods, video games, and Zunes. He claimed that they had to throw the stuff out because the boxes were damaged, even though the ones he brought home were perfect and scratch-free. I didn't question anything he did; I was just happy to have to the stuff. Looking back though, I should've known he was just stealing the stuff and lying to me about how he got it.

It wasn't long before he lost that job as well. A pattern was starting to form with his being unable to hold a job.

We were coming up on our one-year anniversary, and I didn't think it was going to be special since Rocky wasn't working and didn't really have money to do anything. When the day came, he told me to just get cute but prepare to be home. I didn't think anything special could come from not going out of the house. I laid out my clothes before I went to work, and when I got home, he had candles laid out everywhere, soft music playing, and rose petals all over the house. He ordered some pizza, and while we were lying on the couch, he pulled out a letter that told me how much he loved me and how he appreciated everything I was doing for him. It told me to stand up and face away from him, which I did, and he got up and started playing some R Kelly, his favorite artist. He asked me to turn around, and when I did, he was down on one knee. He told me that he had never loved anyone as much as he loved me, and he wanted to know if I would do the honor of being his husband. I cried so much I couldn't speak. I didn't think that I would be getting engaged so young, but I loved him so much I instantly said yes. That was the most romantic gesture anyone had ever done for me. Looked like my luck with love was finally turning around, or so I thought.

A few weeks had passed since the big engagement surprise, and things were getting even better between us; Rocky even got another job. Things were going so well—that is until we had to move out of our apartment into a trailer. The only thing about living in the Earl Homes was that you couldn't have satellite. I wasn't aware of that at the time, but the reason was they didn't want any holes made in the walls. I had the satellite guy come in and make sure everything was neat and clean when he left, and I didn't see how it could be a problem until the landlord came out. I was inside the house while she and the black security officer she was banging were outside looking at the work that was done. "Look at how ghetto this is," she said. I couldn't help but say to myself, "She thinks she is big and bad because she is taking black dick. What does she know about being ghetto?" I was so angry I went outside and let her know exactly how I felt about that comment she'd made. Then she told me that she wasn't going to stand for disrespect and that we had thirty days to find a new place because she was having us evicted. Honestly I didn't care and was glad to move; she wasn't hurting my feelings by no longer taking my money. Rocky was a little mad at the situation, but he said he would've handled it the same way.

We ended up moving into a trailer on the other side of town, and when we moved into that trailer, it seemed his whole demeaner toward me changed. I couldn't figure out what it was; it just seemed like a switch went off in him. He started to spend a lot of time on the computer, and things that he had opened were locked, like his account to the computer.

It was approaching time to pay the bills, and I opened up our phone bill and noticed it was over $400. This was long before the days of smartphones, so there was no logical reason our bill should've been this high. I called the phone company, and it turned out Rocky had been calling sex lines that were charging by the minute. I went into the bedroom and confronted him about it, and when I did, he slapped me to the floor and said I didn't need to be questioning him about anything and to shut the fuck up. I cried and said, "What the hell is wrong with you?" He yelled at me and said that I made him feel bad about himself, and he needed to feel good from someone. "How do I make you feel bad about yourself?" I asked, and he told me since I was working two jobs and in college while he was struggling to keep jobs, it made him feel like he wasn't worth a damn. I told him, "That's your damn hang-up, and don't you ever put your hands on me again, or I'll be gone." I should've just left him then and there with everything I had found out, plus his hitting me.

The very next day, he again lost another job. I didn't even ask what had happened this time around. If there were a record for losing the most jobs in a certain time frame, Rocky would hold it. I couldn't even focus on that, as I was still so angry about what had happened the night prior. My engagement felt more like the engagement from hell. I was still working two jobs at the time and going to school, while he was sitting on his ass browsing the Internet. It wasn't long before the resentment started setting in.

I came home from a long day of working to find that no dinner was cooked and the house was a mess. I asked him what he did all day, even though I already knew the answer to the question. He said, "Nothing. Just browsed the Internet all day."

I was livid at this point. I simply told him, "Get a job, or get out. I don't need anyone in here running up the bills and not even contributing."

Before he could say anything, there was a knock at the door. I went to open it, and it was a girl I used to see at Frigidaire. She was asking if Rocky was home. I said, "I don't know what you are doing here, but now is not a good time," and I closed the door right in her face. I turned to him and said, "Why the hell is she at our house, and how the hell did she know where our house was?" He tried to defuse me by saying she'd told him that she was my cousin and had wanted to come over and see us. "How does that make it better that she is coming to see you and not me then?" Just another thing to sit around and argue about.

For the first time, I wondered if he was bisexual. It would make sense to me: he'd gotten fired from one of his jobs for sexual harassment, and not all of the sex lines he was calling involved men.

There was nothing further he could say to me at this point, and the arguments were going around and around in circles, so it was best that we just take some time apart. I decided to go home to see my family for a few days and let him have the house to himself to think. When I returned home, we decided that we just didn't need to be together anymore. Rocky decided to move back home, and I would keep the trailer. It was a mutual breakup, and I thought that would be the last of the two of us, but I was wrong.

A month after we broke up, right when I started to pick up the pieces of my life, I noticed money started coming out of my bank account. Little amounts at first: five dollars here, ten dollars there, but then larger amounts started to come out. A few days before Thanksgiving, my entire checking account was cleaned out. It was almost $1,000 that came out for purchases on Best Buy and other websites. I had been opening a case with the bank to get my money back, but when they did further investigation into one of the charges, it had a name attached. Apparently Rocky had been using my account to fund his purchases. I reached out to him and let him know that I knew it was him that was doing it. No response from him, but that was only the beginning of my trouble. My e-mail accounts got hacked and deleted. I made another account, and that one was also deleted. My Myspace, Facebook, and bank accounts were all hacked, the passwords changed, and when I tried to recover the information with the security e-mails, I couldn't log in because those too had been hacked. It wasn't just my bank accounts and social media; he also opened bills and credit cards in my name. I think the craziest part of it was that when he got pulled over while driving, he used my name as well.

I had to fight with the police and the creditors to repair the damage done to my credit and my life. I worked with the police department to file charges against Rocky. I had all of the proof, but it didn't seem like the officer I was talking to cared very much about the case, and he didn't do anything to help me. But at least I had the police report to show the banks and all of the credit bureaus to have them remove the charges and close the accounts that I did not open.

Seemed like I had everything taken care of to start repairing my life, until Rocky sent me an e-mail that to this day I still remember. In it, he praised himself for hacking my accounts, and he even told me that from the moment we met, when I'd used his computer, he had all the information he needed to ruin me. He had some type of capture program installed so when I put in my password to check my bank account, it stored it and e-mailed it to him. He was conning me from the start. He told me how much he hated me the entire time we were in a relationship and that it brought him joy when he hit me. So much negativity came out of that e-mail, but one of the things that hurt most was when he said, "You think I cared about you—I didn't. So many times you were at work while I was home getting my dick sucked while you were talking to me on your lunch break. Yeah, that girl that came over to the house was one of the ones sucking my dick while you were working to take care of me."

I was in total shock. I felt the hate steaming from this e-mail. I'm not sure what I did for him to hate me so much; I also didn't want to believe it since we were engaged, and he even had my name tattooed on his arm. Whatever the reason was, his true colors were now revealed: Rocky never cared for me; he was nothing more than a con man who used me to get the things he wanted. It took several years to repair not only the damage he did to my credit and my finances but also my heart. Despite all the drama, I still managed to graduate and decided to continue my education.

4

ME AND YOU, BLACK AND BLUE

After some much-needed time to heal from the damage done by Rocky, I decided it was time to better myself. I enrolled at Lander University in the fall of 2009 and moved to Greenwood, South Carolina, so I could get my bachelor's degree in Political Science. I grew lonely not having someone to talk to at night, so I decided to give love another try. I'd had a few guys message me on Facebook, but since I wasn't ready to date, I'd ignored them. There was one guy, however, who piqued my interest. With Vick, all the signs pointed to "run," but like the fool I was, I decided to ignore them. You see, he had no job at the time, nor did he have a car. Again, my mother always told me, "If you are going to date someone, make sure that they have equal or more than what you have," and yet again I ignored her warning.

Vick was tall, thick where it counted, and had lips that you just wanted to kiss. Seems I'd based all of my relationships on superficial traits, but I knew I wanted to talk to him. We exchanged phone numbers, and things moved insanely fast after that. I'm not sure what it is about the gay community, but it seems like we do things at the speed of light when it comes to relationships. After a few months of dating, Vick and I had already moved in with each other—or should I say he had moved in with me.

Most people's first memory of their relationship is something positive...happy, loving thoughts. My first thought was, "Did this nigga really give me gonorrhea?" Most people would've been smart enough to leave after that, but this book isn't about me always being smart. If good dick makes you stupid, then shouldn't catching the clap make you smart? At least smart enough to realize that this isn't somebody you should be talking to.

If this were a fairy tale, I would say things got better after that, but sadly, this isn't that kind of book. Vick and I dated during the time of the Facebook relationship-killer revolution. Our relationship definitely suffered because he wouldn't stop flirting with dudes on Facebook. Now these dudes were in different states, but that really doesn't matter, as cheating is cheating, whether it be physical or emotional. Several times I had dudes messaging me about him, saying that he was sending them photos of his dick, his ass, whatever they asked for. These dumb-ass dudes actually thought

he cared about them. I remember the first time I con-
fronted him about the messages. The argument was
loud and toxic and so full of lies and denial that I still
to this day don't know the truth. This was the first of
many times to follow that Vick got physical with me.

It's funny when you hear that someone you know
was involved in domestic violence, or when you see it
on TV, and you say to yourself, "I would never let that
happen to me," or "I would do such and such if that
happened to me." I was one of those people who said
that, but when it finally happened to me, I was left feeling powerless. Not only was Vick a liar and a cheater,
but when he got mad, he loved to work out his anger
on my face. Of course, I couldn't tell anyone that this
was going on because this was the man whom for some
crazy reason I was with. So, I lied, covered up the scars,
and cried to myself. I wish I could say that this only
happened once, but sadly this carried on for a course
of three years. I walked on eggshells in my own home
because I didn't know what would happen if I raised
my voice or questioned him about anything.

When Vick finally got a job, it gave him something
to do to keep us separated for a while, even if it meant
him using my car to get to work since he didn't have
one of his own. You would think being a bum would
make you a little more humble, but I honestly think a
part of the reason he was so angry with me was that I
was doing so well for myself and he had nothing going
on. I think he knew I was too good for him, and in

order to feel better about himself, he had to make me feel worse about myself.

One day I decided maybe we should get away and go somewhere, just the two of us, to hopefully bring us closer together. I decided to book a room in Atlanta and drive us there for the weekend. Of course we argued in the car over something crazy, and he decided to punch me from the passenger's side three times to my jaw. I was driving, and it threw me off guard, causing me to swerve into the other lane and almost sideswipe a car. I was so distraught over this, I had to pull off at the next exit and into a Food Lion parking lot.

I asked him, "Why do you have to put your hands on me whenever you get angry?"

His response still rattles me. He said, "Because I can."

This was one of the lowest points of my life, being with a man who claimed he loved me but constantly hit me when he got upset.

We ended up going to Atlanta that weekend despite the arguments and had a pretty decent time, but only because I decided not to push the issue of his hitting me.

Sometime after that, my birthday was coming up, so Vick was being extra nice to me. I never have been big on celebrating my birthday, usually because it always sucked. Normally I was dating some jerk who always seemed to make it about himself instead of about me on the one day I love to celebrate my worth. When

I woke up that day, Vick was being extra nice and sweet to me, waking me with flowers and some birthday sex. Later on, he told me that all I needed to do was to get cute; he had the whole day planned out. He left the house, and I had some time to get all cute for my day. When he returned, he complimented me on how good I was looking and said that he was going to give me one of my birthday presents early. He told me to go get us something to toast with from the fridge, and when I returned, he was down on one knee.

My first thought was, "What the hell are you doing? I hope you don't expect me to marry your crazy ass." Sadly, getting married was always something I wanted to do, and at the time, I thought I was ready for it. My last engagement had been a nightmare, so how could this be any worse than that? "It can only get better," I told myself.

Vick told me how much he loved me and how sorry he was for everything and how he wouldn't let his anger get the best of him anymore. I knew that there was a strong chance that was a lie, but I decided to stay with him, and what was the point of that if I wasn't going to eventually marry him? So, without too much hesitation, I said yes.

After we came down from the high of getting engaged, he took me to my next surprise, which was at this nice hotel. He had planned out a wonderful dinner and even gotten me a birthday cake, something I had told him I'd never gotten from a dude I loved on my birthday. There was a reunion going on upstairs, so the hotel was extremely crowded, but I noticed there was one dude who kept staring over at us. I didn't really pay it any attention because we were gay and we got stared at all the time, so nothing new there. We finished up what turned out to be a very nice dinner—or so I thought, because the next day, I found out who that guy was who was staring at us.

Turns out this dude was somebody whom Vick talked to and who wanted Vick to come upstairs so he could fuck him right in his hotel room. When I found this out, I completely lost my shit. It was yet another instance of where some disrespectful queen was allowed to come in and disrespect our relationship. I wasn't mad at the ho, because that's what hoes do after all; I was mad that Vick was once again talking to any and everything that would pay him some attention. I was so angry, I took his ring and threw it right at him. How was I supposed to marry a guy who was talking to a dude right in front of my face without my knowing it? He looked me right in my face and swore nothing was going on between them and that he would block the guy, but again I asked myself how I could believe he would actually do that.

I started to question myself. Was I ugly? Was my ass not big enough, my dick not big enough? Did I not make enough money to make these dudes happy? I just couldn't figure out what was wrong with me that caused dudes to want to hit me, lie to me, cheat on me.

Or maybe it was something I never got as a child that I tried to search for in the men I dated. This was something I had struggled with for years.

A few months had passed since that incident, and it looked like things were getting back to normal; even the Facebook creeping seemed to have gotten better. Then I decided to go through Vick's phone. He and his friend went to the store, and he left his phone behind. I thought this would be a good time to check and make sure he was still doing good, but I wish I could go back and undo that decision, because the fight that ensued afterward caused something to happen that I will be stuck with for the rest of my life.

When Vick returned from the store with his friend, I tossed his phone at him and said, "So who is this bitch you been texting?"

Like a deer in headlights, he made it seem like I was crazy. Not wanting to get involved, his friend left, but he said he would be back to check on us later. I wish he had stayed, because talking turned into yelling, and yelling of course turned into Vick becoming the Incredible Hulk. He punched me, and I fell down. I got myself up and headed to the bathroom to get some space from him. He ran to the bathroom door, and I could feel him kicking the door to get in. I pressed my back against the door to try to keep him from getting in. It felt like something from a horror movie. I called the police, as I didn't know what this fool was going to do to me if he got through the door.

Finally he stopped trying to kick the door in. A few minutes passed, and I thought he had calmed down a bit. I heard a knock at the front door and thought it was the police, so I headed out of the bathroom. Instead it was Vick pretending someone was at the door so I would come out of the bathroom. When I came out, he grabbed me. I decided enough was enough, and we started fighting. It was fight or become another statistic. I felt like Vick was trying to kill me, and I had to do what I had to do to survive this. I don't remember what happened. I blacked out, and when I came to, I had a three-inch gash down my throat and a one-inch gash on my shoulder blade.

The police finally arrived and separated us. I could barely speak and was trembling in disbelief, thinking about how all of this had just gone down. I didn't really have to say much since I was bruised and bloody. They put Vick in handcuffs and took him off to jail. Never did I want this for him, but maybe this was something he needed to get his shit together.

After the police left, I went to the bathroom, and as soon as I saw myself in the mirror, I started crying. Looking at myself and seeing how badly I was bloodied, bruised, and battered reminded me of a scene in the movie *What's Love Got to Do with It*: the moment right before Tina ran out on Ike—when she was staring at herself in the mirror at how badly she had been beaten. I couldn't let anyone see me this way. What would people think? "What am I going

to tell my mother? How do I hide the scars?" I asked
myself.

While Vick was in jail, I decided enough was
enough. I decided to go and talk to the landlord about
my options to either get out of our lease and move to
separate apartments or kick Vick off the lease and
evict him. I figured the easiest thing would be to ask
for him to move out since I was paying the majority of
the bills and he was using my car to get back and forth
to work, so without it he wouldn't have a job. After he
was released from jail, of course he wanted to apologize for everything, but I wasn't trying to hear that.
After all, I was the one who had to go to class and work
looking like I had survived a UFC fight. I asked—no,
I demanded—that he pack up his stuff and move out.
He refused to do so and yelled that he was on the lease
and the apartment was just as much his as it was mine.
Fearing another argument, I just told him, "Fine, I'll
move out." I had already had the wheels turning on my
own apartment, especially since I had a police report
to show his violence against me to get me out of the
lease. But who needed a police report, when anyone
could just look at me and tell the type of violence I
had been through? I didn't even tell my family this had
happened to me; I didn't go around them either, because I already knew my family would come after him,
and I just wanted this relationship to be done.

Moving day for me was when everything hit the
fan. I couldn't move everything on my own, so I had to

involve my mother and my ride-or-die cousin, Sterling. Vick tried to stop me from taking things that I had used my money to buy, but my mother wasn't having any of that. Luckily, I got all of my stuff out of the house and moved into my new apartment. You would think that would've been the end of this love story, but sadly it wasn't.

Vick and I stopped talking for a while, and I was slowly putting the pieces of my life back together, until he wormed his way back into my heart. I figured since we had been apart for so long that maybe, just maybe, he had changed. He was bringing me gifts and flowers, showing me the love and affection I'd felt I wasn't getting from him during our relationship. I allowed him to come and visit me at my new apartment even though, according to the property manager, we weren't allowed to be around each other because if we had another domestic dispute, we both would be out. I couldn't stay away from this man who hurt me.

Things were going good with us; we didn't put a title on anything this time around because we didn't want the extra pressure of responsibility. Vick was actually acting like the man I fell in love with. I didn't want to tell anyone that we were back talking though. How do you explain that you are talking again to someone who almost sent you to the hospital?

Like all good things though, it eventually came to an end. What was once love and affection quickly turned to anger and jealousy. I refused to make

myself exclusive on his timeline, especially when he
had treated me so dirty, so I still had my dates with
other people. This made him mad once he found out,
which didn't surprise me, but I had made it clear to
him that we weren't rushing back into anything. I told
him that we were just friends and I was free to talk to
and date whomever I wanted, just like he was. The
moment that realization sunk in, the old Vick came
out. We were having a heated conversation, and the
first thing he did was knock me to the floor. This
time was different though. I wasn't going to just lie
down and let him go upside my head. I grabbed the
heaviest object I could get my hands on and hit him
upside his head. He fell down, and I told him to get
the fuck out of my apartment before I killed his ass
like I should've done years ago. He picked up his stuff
and ran for the door.

I noticed something wet running down my face,
so I went into the bathroom and saw that I had a cut
above my eye from where he had hit me. I couldn't do
anything but cry. I had to ask myself, "Galen, is this the
life you really want to live?" Seeing my face like that
again, especially after I had promised myself I would
never let this happen to me again, sent me into a rage.
I must've watched *Waiting to Exhale* one too many
times, because I grabbed everything he'd ever gotten
me and started throwing it on the floor, against the
wall, and down the toilet. By the time I finished, there
was barely anyplace you could step without stepping in

glass. All I could do was lie down in the pile of misery I had created for myself and cry.

This was my fault; I had done this to myself by allowing him to come back in my life. I was done with him. I knew I deserved better, and in order for me to do better, I had to let him and that hurt go. I never really want to say I hate someone, but how else can you say it when that's how you feel? Never would I have thought this cute, thick dude hitting me up on Facebook would turn out to be nothing short of the devil.

5

EVERYTHING THAT GLITTERS

Every time I swear I'm taking a break, it seems like something or someone always throws a wrench into my plans. One day I was working at Chili's; it was a slow day, and I was almost done with my shift, when this guy walked in with a girl and a little boy. I thought the guy was cute as hell, but since he was with them, I really didn't want to stare too much and assumed he was straight. I was cleaning up my area when my coworker called me to the back. She said, "Did you notice how that guy was staring at you?"

I said, "Girl, no, he is not. He has that little boy and that girl with him." But to test it out, she decided to have me take their drinks to them. I walked over and handed them the drinks and figured I would start up a conversation. I can't remember exactly what I said to him, but he made sure to let me know that the girl was his cousin and the little boy was his nephew. He asked me what my name was and what I liked to do. Testing him, I said, "Oh, I don't really do too much around here since I'm new to the area. I'm single, so I don't really go out much."

He told me his name—Chico—and how nice it was to meet me. He said, "Well, how about you write your number down, and we go out sometime?" I had to hide the smile 'cause that was pretty ballsy of him to just flat out ask me, but how could I say no to that?

When I got off work, I texted him, and he set up a date for the next day. I was so excited to have an actual date, as it had been a while since I'd been on one. I put on my tightest pants and my snuggest shirt and stopped by my job to have my coworkers tell me how cute I looked. Chico came by and picked me up from my job, and when he pulled up, I saw what a nice car he had. At the time I was driving an old-ass Kia, so when he pulled up with this brand-new Honda, top of the line, I was real impressed. It was refreshing to be on a date where the guy already had a car and his own money. For me, usually it was the other way around.

We went to the movies. I'm not even sure what movie it was, but one thing I do remember is halfway through, he put his hand on top of mine. Nothing major, but boy was I happy he did that—it made my heart jump, and I started getting those butterflies.

After the movie, he dropped me back off in front of my car. I really wanted to give him a kiss before he left, but I offered to give him a hug instead. He did give me a hug, but he looked like he was nervous about something, and in that moment he told me that he was on the down low and usually didn't do that, but I was something special. Although I enjoyed the hug, I was like, "Oh hell, another damn down-low dude." I didn't have a lot of men flocking to me at the time, so I decided to let it go and see how things would progress.

I had to work that night, but I was still on cloud nine. Chico was still in the area and had been texting me throughout my shift, and he actually said he was going to swing by later that night to see me. Halfway through my shift, there was some crazy drunk man making a scene about having to leave the restaurant. He was getting up in some of the female servers' faces, so I decided to step in between and started pushing him out the door, and before I knew it, the cops came in and snatched him out of the door. I noticed Chico's car was there and decided to go and talk to him since I was so rattled from what had just happened. He wanted to spend more time with me, so he invited me over to his apartment that night when I finished my shift.

When I got off that night, I decided to head to his apartment. I hadn't packed any clothes and smelled like a taco stand, but he said he didn't care, he would give me some clothes and a toothbrush...so I decided to press on. One thing I could appreciate about Chico was that he worked; he had his own car, place, and money, and that was way different from any other guy I had talked to. When I got there and he opened the door, I was looking at him like, "Damn, he is fine." I was so happy that he had invited me over, but I admit I was a tad nervous since we'd only known each other a couple days, and here I was about to spend the night with him. He was so nice and sweet to me though...it made me relax, and I felt right at home.

After I took a shower, we sat on the couch and talked. He gave me my first pair of American Eagle underwear, and he must've liked how I fit in them since he couldn't keep his eyes off my ass. Normally I would be a little offended, but it was cute how he was doing it. We had a wonderful night of just talking. He didn't try to sleep with me or do anything sexual, but he did kiss me. It was one hell of a kiss since he had them soft, big lips, so that was the highlight of my night.

The next day I went home. I had to be up early in the morning, so I took off when Chico went to work. I was feeling pretty special. He had a nice apartment and a good job, which was something I wasn't used to when it came to dating dudes. I usually ended up having more than the dudes I dated, but in this case, we came in having equal things. I had to work both jobs that night, but I was more than happy to ride back to his house after he said he wanted to see me again.

We carried on like this for five days straight, with me going to his house. We spent a lot of time together over the course of the week, and we started to become real close. In fact, after the sixth day, Chico asked me if I wanted him talking to anyone else other than me. I was a little hesitant to answer since it hadn't been that long, but I answered honestly and said, "No, I want you all to myself." He looked at me and smiled and said he didn't want me talking to nobody else either. He said I was special, and he wanted me all to himself. He certainly had a way with words, and I couldn't help the way I was feeling toward him. When he said those words to me, I had to give him some. He took me in the bedroom and definitely put it down. I hadn't had a lot of sex at this point in my life, but I'd had enough to know what I liked and didn't like. Having sex with Chico was magical. He knew how to please me, and he had a kinky side to him that made me feel like we were acting out a porn scene. I got a quick reminder that he was in the closet, however, which led to our first argument.

We went to get his oil changed, and when we pulled up to the place, he got out of the car, looked back, and smiled at me. I waved at him—nothing extra, just a wave—but when he got back in the car, he was so pissed. I looked at him and said, "What's going on with you? Why are you acting like you mad at something?"

He said, "You know I'm not out of the closet. Why are you waving at me like that in public?"

I looked at him like, "Is this nigga serious right now?" Apparently, I'd broken some secret golden rule about dating down low men, so to keep the peace, I decided to apologize. You would think I'd know all of the dos and don'ts of dating a down low man since the majority of my boyfriends seemed to have had some level of down low with them. He told me to just be more careful about what I did when we were out in public. It was hard to get back on the same page that day after that happened, so I decided it would be best if I went home.

I started to notice a pattern forming with Chico: I always went to see him, which was a good forty-five-minute drive from where I stayed. I wanted to get to the bottom of that, so I invited him over to my place. It wasn't in the fanciest of neighborhoods, but I never had any problems, and my neighbors looked out for each other. When he pulled up, apparently my neighbors were looking at him crazy, which made him feel uncomfortable, but he shrugged it off when he came inside, or so I thought. He asked me if his car would be OK out there, and I stared at him like he was crazy. I told him of course it would; nobody like that lives out here. He looked so nervous and told me he had to run out to his car real quick to grab something. When he came back in, he seemed to be a little better, and I didn't think about what he'd actually gone out to get.

He stayed in my apartment for maybe thirty minutes before he turned to me and said, "Would you be mad if we went to my house instead?"

I said, "Yes, I would be mad. You are acting like I live in the hood and somebody is going to lay hands on you."

He offered to put gas in my car if I followed him back to his house. Against my better judgment, and because I actually wanted to spend time with him, I agreed. He filled up my gas tank, and off to his house we went.

It's funny, 'cause in the year we were together, that was the one and only time Chico came to my house.

When we arrived at his house, I was still feeling mad and pretty embarrassed. I felt like I lived in the ghetto and should be ashamed with where I lived. He tried his best to make it up to me that night, but I just really wasn't feeling it. We cuddled up and watched TV until we went to sleep. The next morning, I got up early to leave since I had to go to work.

We had gotten into a routine; I would be home Monday through Wednesday and would be at his house Thursday to Sunday. The more time I spent with him, the more my insecurities started to kick in. Something seemed off about him, but I never could figure out what it was. I started snooping through his stuff to see what I could find because I naturally assumed he was cheating on me. I didn't find anything that stood out to me with cheating, but I did come across something in his phone. He was looking up addictions to pills. I didn't think this was for him—he seemed normal, never seemed like he was high—so I didn't pay that much attention.

Things with our relationship seemed to be OK for a while. For a down low man, he actually spent a lot of time with me outside of the house. He wasn't the typical down low dude where you couldn't go anywhere; he just didn't like showing affection out in public.

He surprised me one day with a trip to Atlanta. I hate Atlanta with a passion, but since we were together, it didn't bother me going. This was the first time we were able to be affectionate in public without his worrying about being judged by someone. We had such a great day that I couldn't wait to get back to his house to show him how much I appreciated him for everything. When we did finally get back, I took extra time cleaning up because I knew this was going to be hot and heavy. When it was time to get started, I wanted to show off my new underwear that I had bought while we were in Atlanta. I was feeling pretty sexy, so I smacked my ass to let him know what time it was. He was not able to get his dick up, however. I asked him what was wrong, as this wasn't something that had happened before, and he told me that when I smacked my ass, it was a turnoff for him because he don't like feminine shit. I didn't even think what I'd done was feminine, but how he said it to me was so disrespectful. I got my stuff and left...drove all the way back home crying because of how he'd spoken to me. He tried to call me, but I didn't want to talk to him for the rest of the night. It was the first time I thought about ending the relationship with him.

On Facebook, he posted a song by Tyrese called "Stay." He couldn't tag me in it since he didn't want anyone to know we were dating, but I knew it was for me. I decided to talk to him when I got up, but honestly, I didn't want to talk about that situation. He apologized, I accepted, and that was all I needed to hear about it.

I decided to return to his house that weekend, which would end up being the last weekend I would be at his house. I missed him, so when I walked through the door, I gave him a big hug and told him that I loved him and that I didn't want to fight anymore over stupid stuff. Things were going pretty good, but slowly throughout the day, it seemed his attitude started to change. He was unnecessarily grumpy over things that I asked him, and he had gotten a phone call that it seemed he wasn't happy about. I asked him who it was, and he yelled, "It's a damn bill collector!"

I looked at him and said, "Who the hell are you yelling at?"

His response was, "I'm yelling at you for asking dumb questions."

I let him know then and there that he wasn't going to be talking to me, and I wasn't prepared for what he said to me next. He actually told me that he didn't want to be with me anymore. I completely shut down after that. I asked him why and where this was coming from. He was so cold toward me and said he thought it was just for the best. As embarrassing as it was for me, I begged him to not do this. "Please, baby, whatever it is, we can work it out," I said. We'd been together for a long time, and I didn't want to have another failed relationship, but nothing I said to him made a difference. I gathered up all of my stuff and ran out of the house crying. I didn't even realize I didn't have my glasses on, I was so upset. I remember that was the longest drive home I'd ever had to make. I had to pull over so many times because I couldn't stop crying. What was usually a forty-five-minute drive took an hour and a half.

How could he do this to me? What had I done wrong, and why now? These were questions that I felt I would never get the answers to. I couldn't work for a few days after the relationship had ended because I couldn't stop randomly crying. Since Chico drove a truck, every time I saw one on the road, I would think about him, get upset, and cry.

A few weeks after he dumped me, I was hoping we were going to get back together. Chico reached out to me and told me he was going to stop by and bring me the things I'd left at his house. I thought this was my chance to get him back, so I pulled myself out of bed, washed away the tears, put on my cutest outfit, and waited on him to arrive. When he came in, he was looking so good...I tried to keep my composure and my tears back, but I couldn't help but break down after I saw him. He asked how I was doing, and I replied, "How do you think I'm doing after being dumped?"

He gave me my stuff and said that he had to tell me something and explain why he'd dumped me. He told me, "Galen, I'm addicted to Oxy."

I stared at him like, "No, you're not. That's just an excuse you are using to spare my feelings."

He informed me that he would take several Oxy a day just to function. At first it was because of his back pain, but eventually it turned into more of an addiction. He also told me that since he was so uncomfortable the day he came to spend the night with me, he went outside and took a few just to calm his nerves. It was taking over his life, and he was going to quit cold turkey. I guess I was wrong when I went through his phone and saw him researching it. I wish I had said something then; maybe it would've helped us somehow. I thought it was for someone else, or maybe I did know it was for him, but true to my craziness, I refused to see the truth that was right in front of me.

Chico told me how sorry he was for hurting me and asked if I could forgive him somehow. I did ask if there was any way we could get back together, now that he was being so honest with me and everything was out in the open. When he told me no, I just didn't understand the reason. I thought love and support were what you needed when you were going through something. Even if he was addicted to pills, why would he still not want to be with me so I could help him? Maybe it was me; he just didn't want to be with me anymore, and he wasn't man enough to tell me that up front. Even though I didn't mean it, I did tell him that I forgave him for the way things had ended. This conversation hadn't gone the way I had hoped.

I decided I'd had enough of feeling sorry for my-self, but more importantly, I'd had enough of these no-account South Carolina men. I needed a fresh start and decided to move to Charlotte, North Carolina to get away, but what I was really doing was running away from my breakup and my problems. I didn't want to see anyone I had dated anymore. I wanted to move as far as possible from all of that pain. A lesson I quickly learned, however, was that men are shit regardless of the area you live in.

Despite what was always going on in my personal life, I never let it interfere with my studies. I graduated from Lander University in August 2011, and with my new degree I wanted to start a new chapter in my life.

6

BALD MAHOGANY GOD FULL OF LIES

A few months had passed since Chico dumped me. I was still making moves to get to Charlotte, but I needed to first find a job. I convinced myself that I wasn't ready to start talking to anyone, but I didn't want to move to a new place and not know anyone either. I told myself I was only going to be looking for friends, but deep down I knew I was lying to myself. I wanted someone to distract me from the pain I was feeling from the breakup. Either way, there was only one thing I wanted to do, and that was to throw myself back out there into the dating world but try to keep it only on a friend level. I needed a rebound to help me get over my ex. I decided to put myself on every dating app I'd ever used and see if anyone was wanting to talk to me. I heard that Charlotte was the

Queen City, a name that had several meanings, and I looked there since that was where I was moving to.

I was pinged by this tall, sexy, bald guy, and when I saw him, I wanted to bang his brains out on the spot. Visually, Mahogany was everything I love to see in a man: tall, muscular, with a nice big dick and an ass for days. Looking back, I knew that was a recipe for disaster, but I didn't care at all because I needed something to help me get over the breakup. Mahogany and I decided to exchange numbers after a few hours of talking online. I came with baggage, and I let that be known from the jump. Usually unloading such information up front scares guys off, but I'm an open book, so anything he needed to know about me, I told him. I didn't want to have anything serious until I relocated to Charlotte, which worked for him, as he didn't like to have long-distance relationships.

A few weeks, sex texts, and Skype calls later, it was time to look for an apartment, which was great for me because I could meet Mahogany in person. I finally found an apartment and completed everything I needed to do, so I stopped by his house to see him. I decided to bring one of my best friends with me since this was my first time meeting Mahogany. When we arrived, I saw Mahogany and another guy sitting on his porch. My first thought when I got out of the car was, "Who the fuck is this bitch sitting in his house?" Mahogany hadn't told me that he was having company over when we spoke. My face said it all. I could've jumped on him the moment I stepped out of the car. We weren't even in a relationship yet, and I was already ready to fight for him. I knew this guy was gay—it was so obvious, the way his thirsty ass was looking at me—but when Mahogany walked up to me, I jumped in his arms and gave him a big-ass kiss. I made sure to make eye contact with the guy on the porch, just to see the facial expressions he made while I was kissing him.

My first question to Mahogany was, "Who the hell is this dude in your house?"

He informed me it was just a friend of his, but with what I now know about him, I know that was a lie. He showed me around his house and didn't mind being affectionate with me, which was nice. He'd been sexy in the photos and the Skype calls, but seeing him in person was on another level. One of the things that turned me on about him was that he had a hard, thuggish appearance, but he spoke with such intellect. Because of that, I wished I hadn't brought my friend with me; I wanted Mahogany to bang me out right in the middle of the living room.

I didn't stay very long because we had to get back home, but I let it be known I didn't like the way his little friend was staring at me. There was a time in my life when, if a dude looked at me funny, we ended up fighting. I was trying to turn over a new leaf, so kicking ass didn't need to be a part of my new-me attitude. When I was halfway back home, Mahogany called me and said that the guy was trying to sleep with him after

I left and was questioning him about who I was. But he stated that he didn't sleep with the guy and told the guy to get out after he tried to push up on him. It took everything in me not to make a U-turn and find that dude and fuck him up for what he'd done. However, I bought into that bullshit Mahogany fed me, thinking he was so nice and sweet and honest for telling me that.

After meeting with him and getting my apartment, I wanted to move as soon as I possibly could so he and I could be together officially, so I boxed up the rest of my stuff and moved to Charlotte in January 2012. I hadn't been there long before the real drama started for me. It was Valentine's Day and my first day on the job, and all I could think about was getting off and spending time with Mahogany. I had my bed being delivered that day, and I just kept thinking about breaking it in the moment he came through the door. The delivery guys called me when I was on my way home. They said they were there waiting on me, so I had to floor it to get there and set everything up before Mahogany got off.

I finally got to the apartment and greeted the movers. They seemed nice, and we had a casual conversation. Again, I'm an open book, so when one of the guys asked me if I had any plans for Valentine's Day, I told him I had just moved there, and I couldn't wait until my boyfriend got off since it was our first Valentine's Day together. After I said that, I noticed how he followed me with his eyes when I walked around the apartment. It was extremely obvious that he was staring at my ass, but I was so focused on trying to set up my V Day surprise that I didn't pay much attention to what was going on. After the bed was finished, they informed me I had to sign the proof that it was delivered and set up. Then both of them went out the door, but the one who was looking hard came back in. While I was signing the paperwork, he asked me, "Oh, so you waiting on your boyfriend, huh?"

I replied, "Yeah, I am. It's our first Valentine's Day together, so I'm excited."

He looked at me and said, "I bet your boyfriend don't have a big dick like I do. Now let me see how you suck it."

This crazy-ass dude proceeded to unzip his pants, pull his dick out, and start walking toward the bed that he'd just set up. I was completely frozen; the only thing I could think of was when I was raped by my ex. I didn't know what to do or say in that moment. I don't remember how much time passed before I was able to speak; the fear had taken over my body and paralyzed me. Finally, I snapped out of it and told him to get the hell out of my house before I took a knife and cut that dick clean off his body and shoved it down his throat. He put his dick back in his pants and quickly ran out the door. The first thing I did was break down and cry. That moment took me back to a part of my life I thought I had gotten over. It's funny...when you think you've gotten over something, all it takes is one thing to trigger those emotions and send you right back to that dark place.

After I got myself together, I called Mahogany and told him what had happened to me. He got so angry I didn't know what he was going to do, but the first question he asked me was if I did what the guy asked me to do. I was so offended that he would even ask me that question, especially with the fear I had in my voice when I was explaining to him what had happened. All I could think about was, "Some Valentine's Day this is turning out to be." My first real experience in Charlotte was getting flashed by a pervert who wasn't even cute and having the man I was with question my morals.

Mahogany finally showed up at my house, and I was just so happy to see him I didn't even notice the flowers in his hand. He kissed me and said he was so sorry about what had happened to me and he would never let anyone hurt me that way again. He also apologized for questioning me about the situation, which was better than any gift he could've given me. The night actually got a lot better after he got there. We had sex for hours on the new bed, on the old bed, and everywhere in between. Sex with him was magical. As bad as this sounds, he was experienced and knew what to do and where to do things. He asked if I trusted him, which I did, so we didn't use condoms. Another prime example of not using my best judgment, but it just felt so good, at least at the time.

When I woke up the next morning, Mahogany was already gone. He worked an early shift, so I hadn't expected him to be there when I got up, but he left a letter saying that he loved me and for me to call him when I got up. I was feeling so good, on top of the world from that marathon lovemaking we'd had. I couldn't believe how good I felt the next day and how happy I was—that is, until I took my first piss of the morning. I felt the most horrible burning sensation I've ever felt in my life, and I yelled at the top of my lungs the moment the urine exited my body. I was in so much pain I didn't know what to do. I looked down at my underwear and saw white and green stains. I named that experience the "piss heard 'round the world," because a few minutes later, I had the police knocking on my door asking if I was all right. Apparently, the neighbors had heard me yelling and thought I was being attacked.

I went back into the bathroom and took a look at my dick. There was so much discharge coming out of me. As embarrassing as it was to have the police called on me, I had bigger problems going on. I made the first available appointment to see a doctor. I'd had gonorrhea once before, so I knew what it felt like, but this was a whole other experience. I didn't want to tell Mahogany what was going on until I knew exactly what it was. Last thing I needed to do was accuse him before I had my receipts to prove my case. I knew what it was, and I knew whom I'd gotten it from, but just so there would be no confusion or way to deny anything, I wanted proof to take.

At my doctor's appointment, the moment I pulled down my pants and the doctor took a look at all of the green sludge dripping out of my dick, she said, "You appear to have gonorrhea." She told me that usually they have to stick the swab in your penis to get the sample, but since the discharge was coming out with such volume, she just had to swab up against my dick to get it. Officially she couldn't say it was gonorrhea until the results came in, but off the record, she was fairly certain of what it was.

I couldn't get out of that office fast enough to go to Mahogany's house and rip his head off, but I decided to wait until the results came in. I pretended everything was fine with me for what felt like an eternity while I was waiting on my results. Sex was completely out the window, but my unavailability didn't stop him from having it with other people. I was in day three of waiting on the results to come in, but lucky for me, the medicine the doctor had given me started to alleviate some of my symptoms. Mahogany had had a rough day at work, so to keep up appearances, I decided to go over and try to make him happy. I spent a few hours over there before he decided to try to have sex with me. I had to come up with an excuse as to why I couldn't. I told him that my stomach was hurting, which is a usual excuse bottoms use to get out of sex, but he wasn't taking that answer well. He got extremely mad and actually told me to leave because he didn't feel like having an argument about my not wanting to give him some. I left and waited a few hours before I called him. He didn't answer, so I kept calling.

It was early in the day when I started to call him, and several hours later there was no answer, no texts, and no return call. I decided to pop up at his house. His car was in the driveway, and I knew he was in there because I heard noises, and the living room lights were on. The voices got louder, so I started knocking on the door. Knocking turned to banging because I felt this bitch had another dude in his house. I stood outside his house for twenty minutes knocking on his windows and his doors, and he never came to let me in. I got in my car and left to head back home, and when I was halfway home, he finally decided to call me and ask why I was knocking on his door. I cussed him out for everything that he was worth, which wasn't much, and hung up the phone. I still didn't mention the fact that I'd been to the doctor to get tested.

The next day my results finally came in. Not only did I have gonorrhea, but I also had chlamydia. I wasn't even aware you could have both at the same time, but that definitely explained why I was in such pain. "Coinfection" was what the doctor called it. Luckily my HIV test came back negative; having two STDs was bad enough, but having HIV would've been the final nail on the coffin for Mahogany.

I was like a dog with a bone when it came to showing him those results. The time couldn't pass by fast enough for him to get off work so I could rush over there and confront him. I was already pissed about the previous night, so that was the first thing to be discussed. When I pulled up, he was sitting on the porch. I had my letters in my pocket ready to show, but I decided to hold off till the end before I threw that in his face. I got out, gave him a hug, and said, "So what happened last night?" He claimed he was asleep and hadn't heard anything. I looked him dead in his face and said, "You are a liar. I know you had another bitch in your house, so if you are going to tell me a lie, you need to make it a better one than that." He kept arguing with me, saying that I was crazy and being paranoid, and he refused to acknowledge any wrongdoing on his part. "I heard the dude moaning from your bedroom," I stated. Again, nothing but denials from him.

I'd had enough of his bullshit and his attitude, so I told him he could kiss my ass and go straight to hell and take his STDs with him. I threw the papers in his face and walked back to my car and peeled out of his driveway. Within thirty seconds he called me, asking why I didn't tell him I had that and wanting to know whom I got it from, because I didn't get it from him. I knew that was a lie because I'm not the type to mess around like that, and my symptoms had started the day after we had unprotected sex. I hung up on him. I was over the whole conversation. He called back, and I sent him to voice mail. He kept calling me over and over, so after about thirty missed calls, I decided to call him back.

This liar tried to say that maybe it was possible one of us had had the STD for several months and just didn't have any symptoms until recently. He also tried to blame me, saying that maybe I actually slept with that mover who showed me his dick and lied about what actually happened that day before he came over. That insinuation made me realize that this relationship was done. Even though we hadn't discussed a lot of my past, he knew that I had experienced a trauma and that I was afraid of being placed back in that situation again. He even claimed he had a friend who worked as a nurse who said you can have those STDs for several months without showing any signs, so maybe one of us had had it and didn't know. I am no idiot, and I knew that was complete bullshit.

I decided to take a much-needed break from him and the failing relationship. We just had too much negativity going on. We didn't speak for a week before he reached out to me and told me how much he missed me. I knew I should've been done with him after the STD fiasco, but he was so sexy, and I was lonely, so I decided to invite him over so we could have a face-to-face conversation. Although he didn't admit any wrongdoing, he did apologize for how things had played out between the two of us.

GALEN J. CROMARTIE

After he left, I started thinking about how seriously I wanted to take this relationship, because he just didn't seem to think he'd done anything wrong. As much as I hated to admit it, another part of me didn't want anyone getting that magnificent dick or ass but me—even though it was obvious that someone had been or was getting it behind my back since we'd started dating.

He called to check on me later that night, which I thought was sweet, but right before we got off the phone, right after he said he loved me, I heard the infamous Adam4Adam hookup notification sound. Before he hung up, I stopped him and said, "What was that sound?"

He said, "Oh, that was nothing but my Microsoft notification sound."

I was like, "Is this boy crazy?" Clearly he'd forgotten that I worked in IT and knew that Microsoft doesn't have a sound like that. Plus, of all the excuses he could've given, was that really the best one he could think of? The Adam4Adam sound is so distinctive, any gay man knows it when he hears it. I honestly didn't have the energy to argue with him anymore about anything else. I knew what I'd heard, and I let that be that.

I had a mental breakdown that night. I couldn't figure out what was wrong with me that I allowed myself to be so stupid, because I knew what Mahogany was doing, what he had done, and yet I continued the cycle with him. I had come to ignore a lot of the signs that a smarter person would've run away from. Were his sex game and good looks really strong enough for me to put myself through all of this?

Mahogany came over the next day, and I had one thing on my mind: going through his phone to see what he had really been doing when we were not around each other. I already knew he had been doing something, but until I saw it for myself, I wouldn't believe it. I had to be strategic with everything though, because he didn't leave his phone sitting around ready to be looked through. I decided to use sex as my weapon and put it down on him so badly that he needed a shower afterward. While he was in the shower, I looked in his phone; he didn't have a password on it, so that made things a lot easier for me. I saw where he was sending photos of his ass and his dick to four different dudes and giving them directions to come over and get fucked—conveniently, the same night he didn't come to the door when I was trying to get him to answer me. The dots started connecting for me as to how I'd caught my coinfection and whom I'd caught it from.

When he got out of the shower, I threw the phone at him, yelling about how he had been cheating on me, and now he was caught right in the act with no way to lie out of it. He couldn't say anything. He tried to get mad at me for going through his phone, but I shut that down right away and kicked him out of my house. I told him we were through and I wanted nothing more to do with him. I was upset, of course, but I felt so much better not having to worry about him anymore.

He tried to lure me back in by saying that he had bought an engagement ring and was going to propose to me. We had talked about getting married in the general sense, but I hadn't thought it would come so soon. I knew he was just saying that so I would talk to him, which, sadly, I ended up doing again. I met with him about a week after we broke up because he kept apologizing and said he would do anything to get me back. He swore he never actually met up with anyone he was talking to and it was just a dumb mistake. I told him the only way I would take him back would be if he changed his number, did not put a passcode on his phone, and promised me that he would never do it again. If he cheated on me again, he was to never try and contact me again. He agreed to everything. Even though we had only been together for a few months, I didn't want to lose him permanently, and since he didn't want me moving on, he agreed to the things I stated.

Things got back to normal for a while. We were getting close, and I was falling in love all over again. Sometimes going through something like this makes you grow closer together as a couple, but only if the relationship survives what happened. I will admit I loved the look of jealousy I would get from the other gay men when we went out on a date. Of course, that also could've been a look of "I'm sleeping with your man, and you're too dumb to realize it."

I invited Mahogany over to celebrate our being together for half a year, and I wanted to do nothing but
drink, eat, watch TV, and of course have sex. I hadn't
gone through his phone since we started dating again;
I honestly didn't want to because a huge part of me
knew he hadn't really changed, and I knew that I was
going to find something when I looked. But that night
I decided to look. He got drunk off beer and passed
out while we were watching *Cheaters*, which is truly the
definition of irony. While he was asleep, I grabbed his
phone off the table and looked through it. I found out
that he was still on his Adam4Adam page and that he
had still been sending nude photos of himself all over
the Internet to any and every dude who would pay him
a compliment. I couldn't do anything other than cry.
How could this be happening to me again? He'd sworn
he wouldn't do it again, and yet here we were.

I woke him up and just started yelling and accus-
ing. True to his form, he denied everything and actually had the nerve to say that one of his friends was
using his phone, and he let this friend use the profile,
but he hadn't actually been on it himself. It seemed he
was really good at making shit up. I didn't want to hear
any of his bullshit this time around, and I told him to
get the fuck out of my house. He started to get his stuff
since he saw how angry I was getting, and as I opened
the door to let him out, he pushed me into my TV. I
fell, and some things from the shelf fell on top of me. I
don't know what came over me, but I decided to shove

him back and again repeat, "Get the fuck out of my house." Next thing I knew, he swung and hit me in my jaw. Here we went again, another man thinking that it was OK to put his hands on me.

I'm not sure what came over me, but I told myself, "Never again." I would never let a man put his hands on me and think he could get away with it. I went into the kitchen, and he followed, pushing me into the stove this time. He took another swing and hit me in the stomach. I went down and grabbed the first thing I saw from the cabinet, which was a cast iron skillet. I took a swing and hit him upside his head. I was in a furious rage and just yelled, "Get out, or I'll kill you!" I kept swinging, hitting him in the back as he ran toward the door, a trail of blood following him across my carpet. I wasn't thinking about going to jail, what would happen if the police came, or anything that could get me into trouble. All I could think about was surviving, not being another statistic dead on the ground because of some idiot and his poor choices. Finally he reached the door and ran to the car. I chased him and threw the skillet at his car as he was driving away, but I missed. I grabbed my skillet off the ground and ran back into the house and closed the door.

It took what felt like an eternity for all the adrenaline I was running on to calm down. Once that settled, all I could do was cry. I could not believe I had gone through this again. "Why did you take him back?" I asked myself. I knew what kind of dude he was, and yet I'd decided to push that aside and keep talking to him. "You deserved this," I told myself as I spent hours putting myself down and blaming myself for what had happened. How was I going to go to work with this bruise on my face?

Of course he had broken the agreement, but he reached out to me again, saying how dumb I was and that I would regret what I'd done to him. I was so scared he would come back to my apartment and re-taliate or do something crazy that I didn't leave out the house unless I had to. I had friends spend the night with me because I was scared to be alone—not the best way to live, for sure. I threatened that if he ever came over to my house unannounced, I would shoot his dick off right back to wherever it was that he came from. He never contacted me again after that, but the damage he did to me will always be there. Sad thing is we only dated for a couple months, but with all the drama it felt like so much longer.

I needed to take a long break from dating anyone after that, and the scariest thing was that I had to get a ton of STD tests just to make sure he didn't give me anything else. Thankfully everything came back clean.

7

BBB (BROKE BUM BITCH)

After another failed relationship, I decided I didn't want to date anyone for a while. I focused on myself, work, and making new friends to fill the void. Sex was out of the question for a while since I had to get tested regularly until I was past the window when anything that I might have caught from Mahogany would possibly show up. I was doing pretty well getting to know myself all over again, but eventually I got bored and lonely, and I thought I would give online dating another try.

I usually try to stick to dudes in my area, as I tend to be needy at times, and long-distance relationships usually don't work out for me. I got a message from this light-skinned guy who looked pretty cute in his pictures. One thing that stood out to me was how masculine and big he appeared, like a teddy bear. That's probably one of my biggest weaknesses, a nice fluffy guy who can carry his weight. When he messaged me, he was definitely talking to me in a way that I liked. He was living in Boston, which was a good ways away from me, but he said that he was planning on moving back to Charlotte since he used to live there once upon a time.

As time passed, we started to get closer and closer. I think one good thing about having a long-distance relationship with someone is that communication is all you have. You have to talk to the person and really get to know him since you aren't physically with him. A night would not pass without us doing video chat. We even started to get a little kinky with it and started having Skype sex, which he seemed to love. BBB loved to send me text messages just to let me know he was thinking about me and sweet little poems to let me know he cared.

We talked about seeing each other a lot since we had been talking to each other for a few months. I was worried about making that long drive; he didn't have a car of his own, so he couldn't come and see me. True to my superhero complex, I had this mind-set of "I can fix him up and shape him into what I want him to be." I decided I wanted to go and see him, but this was a sixteen-hour drive and the longest drive I had ever done on my own. I was working in a not-so-high-paying job, so money was also going to be an issue. I had asked him if he could chip in for some gas money since I was the one doing the driving, but of course he came up with some excuse about how he was so broke at the time. But it was fine...well, fine but not really fine. Anyway, I decided to go ahead and make the drive. At least I could stay with him and make the most out of our time together.

I took some time off work and hit the road. After what felt like an eternity, I made it to him and was ready to get me some sleep. He wasn't what I was expecting when I saw him, as he looked real different from his photos and the Skype videos. I guess RuPaul must've rubbed that Vaseline on the lens, because this guy really didn't look the same. Not ugly but just not as cute as I was expecting, especially after driving sixteen hours. I told him how tired I was and that I needed to take a nap, but he said, "Oh. Well, we are going to have to get a hotel." Oh, did I forget to mention he was living with his mother at the time? I was down for getting a room though, as I did plan on getting some from him and didn't need or want his mother walking in on us.

I didn't know the area, so I let him drive us to the hotel. When we got there, I was looking at him to pay or contribute, but he had no money. I had to pay $200 for this room, which was money I hadn't anticipated spending. I was so angry and sleepy at this point that all I wanted to do was go to sleep, but I could tell he wanted to get him some, and that usually takes the anger out of me, so I decided to strip down and take him around the world. The sex with him was wack to say the least and definitely not worth a sixteen-hour drive. I was in a rush to nut just so I could be done with it and get some sleep.

Later that night he wanted to take me to one of his favorite bars, where he usually got a hookup, and believe it or not, I didn't have to pay for anything. Probably because he knew the owner. Seems like I can't go anywhere with a dude without there being some kind of drama involved, because this dude BBB used to talk to was there. But I never let a bitch see me sweat, so I was all nice to the guy. He kept throwing little digs at me about BBB, but I kept letting things slide. That was until he said something about where I come from, and I jumped up in his face and told him, "This South Carolina dude is about to whoop your little ass." At that time security ran up on us and caught me midjump as I was coming across the table on him. Since BBB knew the owner, he convinced the owner to kick the dude out of the bar, and I got to stay in and keep on partying. I guess seeing that side of me must've turned him on, because we left not too long after for round two of our sex. It was a little better the second time around, but sadly, not by much.

I really wasn't too happy during the whole trip, as I felt like the man I'd come to see couldn't help finance the trip that he wanted more than I did. A smart person probably would've let that be the end of the relationship, but again this book isn't about me being smart.

After the slightly better sex, we went to sleep. It had been a long night, and I was leaving in the morning. Again no gas money was offered to me for my sixteen-hour drive back to North Carolina, and I gave BBB a hug and a kiss and hit the road. I had a long ride home to think about what I wanted out of our relationship, and I wasn't sure that he was it. I had to ask myself what it was I was doing with my life. I'd just made this long drive to see someone that I had only been talking to online and through Skype. He fit the same mold as all of my other exes, just in a different package.

A few weeks had passed since I'd gone to visit BBB, and things weren't the same for us. It wasn't just me though; he seemed to have been spending more time going out at night and less time having our usual Skype sessions. At first, I didn't care much, as I was still pretty pissed off about having to fund our visit, but we had been in a routine, and I started to miss it. We started to argue a lot as well about dumb things. Could be over my going to work, the clouds in the sky—any dumb thing really. Seemed like the more we talked, the more we argued.

My birthday was coming up, and it was time for my annual Orlando trip. I usually go every year, and I was looking forward to some time away from all the arguing and bickering. Unfortunately, BBB felt that since he was my boyfriend, he was entitled to go with me to spend time with me on my birthday. I really didn't want him to come along because at this point I'd really started to hate him.

A few weeks before my birthday, he decided to drop a bombshell on me, saying that he had decided to go ahead and move back to Charlotte before his original move date, so now he would be moving the week after my birthday. Also, he had left his job to start focusing on packing up his stuff to move down and live with his family. He asked if he could borrow $300 so he could come with me to Orlando and spend time with me but still have money to get me something and to spend on his own. I really didn't want to give him anything, let alone my money, but I'm always so nice and giving in relationships with people who aren't worth a damn. I agreed to give him the money but said he had to pay me back the moment he got his job in Charlotte and on his first check. He managed to get a car to drive down to Charlotte to meet me, which was good because I wasn't going there to pick him up. We left for Orlando not too long after he had arrived. We drove together to Orlando—in my car, because what he had was a rental that he had to take back. From the moment he got in the car till the time we got to Florida, we argued.

We finally arrived in Florida on my birthday, and of course I wanted to be cute. I had on some tight, dark jeans, a nice black shirt, some jewelry, and my nicest shades. We decided to go to the mall, and since it was my day, I figured I could dress and act however I wanted. When we got to the mall, he turned and looked at me, asking, "Why you walking around with your sunglasses on like you're all that?"

I was like, "Well, it is my birthday. If I'm not allowed to feel all that on my day, then when can I?"

The whole day, he treated me like shit, and once again I wasn't happy on the one day I feel can be about me. He went into Ecko, which was a store back then, and bought my birthday gift—a watch. I didn't even wear watches, he never saw me with a watch on, and yet he bought me a watch. Matter of fact, I bought myself a watch since he was using my money to buy the gift. I hated the watch; it looked like something you would get from a gas station in the hood. I just smiled and said thank you and kept it moving. My birthday was shaping up to go down as one of the worst ones I'd ever celebrated. Dinner was the highlight of my night, not because I had a great time with the man I was dating but because we went to a TGI Fridays that was right across from Universal Studios. It was Total Nonstop Action (TNA) wrestling night, and all the wrestlers came over after the event, and I got to meet a lot of wrestlers I grew up watching as a kid.

After dinner we went back to the hotel. I guess the only other thing to be happy about was having sex at this point. I was drunk, so I wanted to get some, but BBB didn't really seem to be in the mood, for whatever reason. He decided to go get some ice so we could keep on drinking. He was gone for about fifteen minutes just to go get some ice right down the hall. When

he came back through the door, he was all over me—
he started ripping my clothes off. I looked at him and
was like, "Why are you so excited all of a sudden?"

He said, "I just saw someone real attractive out in
the hallway, and it got me horny."

I could've slapped the pure dog shit out of him,
and if I hadn't been so drunk, I probably would've. I
decided to let it pass for that moment because I really
wanted some, but you better believe we were going to
circle back to the comment when I regained my senses.
Again, the sex was wack. I just had to realize that sex
with this dude was never going to be good. The only
thing he could do half good was suck dick, and even
that wasn't great. Picture that: a gay man who can't
suck dick good.

After we finished, I pushed him off me and turned
over. He asked me what was wrong and if I'd enjoyed
it. I should've been a real bitch and said, "Hell, no," but
I decided to say, "I'm tired and drunk and just want to
go to sleep."

But, being the ass he was, he said, "No, you are going to talk to me now and tell me what's wrong."

The rage I'd been feeling all day finally came out
on him. Drunk and all, I let him know exactly how I
was feeling about that slick comment he'd made. After
I'd called him every possible name in the dictionary, he said, well, I could just send him home back to
Charlotte. I was like, "Oh, so now you want me to pay
for you to go back to Charlotte, after I paid to have you

here. What a bum bitch—you can't even afford to send yourself home because you didn't have any money to come here to begin with."

This was the last straw for me. There was no way I could continue a relationship with someone like this. It's one thing to argue and have a shitty boyfriend with some good dick, but when you don't even have the stroke game to back up your crazy, it's definitely not worth it. I cut my birthday trip short because I couldn't take being with him in that cramped hotel for another day. After the argument we went to sleep, woke up, and hit the road. I couldn't wait to get back to Charlotte. We both knew the relationship was dead, and there was no need to try to fix it. We didn't say a word to each other the entire ride back home. I think, had he said anything smart to me, I would've kicked him out of the car on the highway.

I was so glad he moved in with family and not with me. I couldn't imagine living with this dude. I let him know I didn't want anything to do with him, but he needed to pay me my money back. Being as petty as he was, he said he wasn't paying me anything back because, since I made all that money, I didn't need the money paid back to me. That sparked another argument, but it went nowhere. The way that he was talking to me was like he resented me for making the money I was making. I wasn't even making anything back then that would warrant such aggression. He was a complete ass, and he used me—there is no other way to put it.

A few months had passed, and I started to move on and go out on dates with some other guys. Since we hadn't dated long, there was no love lost between me and BBB and nothing for me to get over. I hadn't thought about him since we broke up, but he found me and messaged me. The only reason I responded was because I was hoping to get my money back from him. Not because I needed it but because I deserved it.

We decided to meet back up. I knew it would be a mistake bringing him back around me, but he was making it hard to not want to forgive him. He must've felt bad for the way things had ended. He started leaving me gifts outside my door for me to see when I would leave to go to work. Not sure where he was getting the money to leave me those gifts, but it was a nice gesture that no other guy had ever made for me. It's hard to stay mad at somebody making such a gesture to win your affection back. I decided to build a friendship again with him, something I thought we'd had before but actually hadn't. My definition of being friends, however, is being able to tell the friend when he or she is acting like an asshole. I couldn't tell him that though. We had another big argument, and for the life of me, I can't remember what it was about.

I wanted nothing to do with him at this point, and when he decided to ping me on A4A, I decided to just flat out block him. When I did that, he decided to write me and say, "I am so glad I released you. I was being nice, sending you a smile, and you blocked me—wow.

One day, Galen, I hope you understand that you are a horrible human being. You treat people like shit and you talk to them like they're nothing. You're just a horrible piece of flesh, and the sad part is that you need a counselor to pretty much tell you what a waste of skin you are. One day you are going to meet your match, and when you do, you will regret it."

My first thought was, "You no-count, no-job-having bum-ass bitch, you had the audacity to come for me when you didn't have the money to come with me to Florida and bummed three hundred dollars from me so you could go and 'spend money' but never paid me back."

There was no response needed to his message. Although I had so much I could've hit him back with, sometimes the best response and revenge is to do nothing at all. So that's what I did, nothing. I decided to block him and remove all traces of him from my life. I deleted his number, blocked him on all of the social media and dating apps, and removed all the pictures from my phone. I was done with him. The funny part was that I'd thought bringing him back around would get me my money back, but still to this day, I have never gotten back the money that he owed me, and I never will.

8

MR. CODEPENDICK

One boring day I decided to get on Facebook and start adding a bunch of random dudes who were in my area and who I thought were cute. I came across this one profile with this guy, Ray, whom I was instantly attracted to. I decided to send him a friend request, and he approved, and within a few minutes we were chatting about some random things—nothing too serious. We decided to exchange numbers, and we spent the entire night texting, which was something I hadn't done in a long time. He asked me out on a date for the next day, and before I could even think about it, I said yes. When I tell you this dude was fine, I mean he had the kind of lips you want to kiss, the sexiest eyes, and that sexy caramel skin I loved. Before we went to sleep, he said the sexiest thing to me. He said, "Call Ray and tell me good night." I don't know what it was about that text that got me hot and bothered, but it did. I called him, and his voice was just the final thing that made me get extra excited about our date. He had the kind of voice that would make you want to have phone sex. He could read the dictionary to me, and I would get turned on. He told me that he was looking forward to meeting me and seeing what I was about.

The next day came, and I knew I had to be cute for this date. I don't remember a time when I was more excited to meet someone. I decided to put on my pants that usually got a lot of stares and a tight shirt with one of my baseball hats. I pulled up to Ray's house, and when he walked out, it was something out of a movie; everything was in slow motion, and I was staring at this dude like, "Wow, he actually looks better in person than in any photo I've seen of him." I got out to give him a hug but wasn't trying to come off so desperate.

I wanted to see a scary movie; that way when I got scared, I could cuddle up next to him. I don't remember what movie it was—it could've been *Sesame Street* for all I cared—I was just happy to be out with this guy. Ray was the perfect gentleman. He opened all the doors for me, and he even held my hand while we were out in public. There is nothing sexier than a masculine man who isn't afraid to show some affection to you while you are out with him. He opened the doors that led to our seats, and I walked in front of him but turned around to notice him staring at my ass. When I looked up and smiled, he grabbed my hand, pulled me to him, and kissed me. My knees buckled, and I almost fainted, because when I say that Ray could kiss, I mean he had lips that could suck a golf ball through a garden hose.

After he finished kissing me, he looked at me and said, "I'm sorry, I just had to do that."

I told him, "Don't apologize. I didn't mind it at all."

When the movie finished, I asked him if he was ready to go home, secretly hoping he would say no because I wanted Ray with me for the night. He told me that he wasn't ready and asked if we could keep hanging out throughout the day, so we decided to head back to my apartment to get better acquainted. Now a smart person wouldn't take a person he'd just met back to his house, but shoot, I was willing to risk it for this dude.

When we got back to my apartment, we decided to sit on the couch and tell each other more about ourselves. I didn't want to immediately tell him everything about me—not the bad parts anyway. He did, however, tell me some things about him—not great things either. I found out that he didn't have a job at the time (seemed like a pattern for me to keep dating unemployed people), but he was getting some assistance from the government because he was schizoaffective. I had no idea what that meant, but he watered it down for me and said that sometimes his mood went from happy to sad but it didn't get him down to where he couldn't lead a normal life. I didn't really see it as a problem at the time since we were just talking and getting to know each other.

Ray was so affectionate with me, and that was something I hadn't gotten from my last relationship. I think that is a big part of the reason that I decided to give him a chance. We nixed all the emotional talk and just kept it light for the rest of the afternoon. I decided to ask him to spend the night since we were having such a good time—and I was a little horny too, so I decided to see if I could get some while he was there. We headed toward the bedroom and did some foreplay, which was incredible, but when he pulled down his pants and I saw what he was working with, my first thought was, "Holy shit, how am I going to take all that?" Fortunately, we decided to hold off on the full sex and stick with the foreplay.

The next day I dropped Ray back off at home. He didn't have a driver's license or a car, so that was something I had to decide if I wanted to deal with. We kept in touch and actually started catching feelings for each other pretty quickly. We also spent just about every day with each other. What I fell for the most about Ray was that he was so nice, and he was incredibly sexy but not arrogant about it. My superhero complex really kicked in with him. I knew that if I could help get him work and get him driving, he would be the perfect guy for me. These were things that I shouldn't be thinking when dating someone; if I had my things together, so should the person I chose to be with, but for whatever reason I was constantly drawn to guys who weren't the total package.

A few months passed by. Since Ray was living with his brother but wasn't getting along with him, I decided to move him in with me after he asked me if I wanted to take it to the next level. I honestly don't know why I wanted him to live with me. I think I was just tired of being alone, and since things were going really good between us, I took a leap of faith.

Ray was attentive, faithful, and sexy, and I felt happy and complete with him. Things between us were going great. I had not only a boyfriend but an amazing friend whom I was building a life with. That was, until his schizoaffective side kicked in. When he had those days, it was, "Oh, I'm not sure if I want to be in a relationship," and, "Oh, how I miss being in my home state." It started to seem like every month we had to have a conversation about whether he wanted to be with me. Who wants to be in a relationship like that? But God, that dick was so good, I just didn't want to let him go.

One day I came home, and he was sitting on the chair. He looked like he had a lot on his mind, so I asked him, "What's wrong?"

He said, "Hey, baby, sit down. I've got something I want to tell you. I know we have been dating for about six months now, and I realize that I love you and can trust you. I have been wanting to tell you this for a while now, but I just didn't know how. I didn't want to

scare you off and ruin the good thing that we have going on. You are my life, and I can see a future with you,
so here goes. I'm a convicted felon."

I looked at him and was like, "I'm sorry, say what?
You've got to be kidding me, right? There is no way
that this could be true."

He started to tell me the stories, but I couldn't
believe that this was accurate, so I googled him, and
there were his mugshots. I was in a state of disbelief.
"What do I do in this case? And good Lord, what have
I gotten myself into?" I thought. I would think this is
the kind of thing you tell someone in the beginning
of the relationship to let them decide if they want to
continue to be in a relationship with you. Not when
they have become so heavily invested in the relationship. I'll be honest, a part of me felt like I was dating
someone a little dangerous, and that was a turn-on for
me. His crimes didn't involve murder or selling drugs,
so I didn't think it was that big a deal. Plus, these were
things that had happened prior to his meeting me,
and I'm no saint, but definitely no criminal either. I
decided to just keep moving forward with him. I appreciated the honesty because I probably wouldn't have
found out about it if he had not told me the truth.

Ray wasn't working when I met him, but he was getting a check from the government since they felt he
couldn't work. Before we officially moved in together,
we sat down and discussed how much of his check
would go toward bills. He didn't get a lot of money on

his checks, but it was enough to pay all of the bills except for the rent. For the first few months, he gave me the money on time and without any trouble. Then I noticed when it was time to pay the rent, he sometimes didn't have his money. I know he didn't have any other bills outside of his phone bill, but I couldn't figure out where his money was going. He would tell me that he had to give his mother or his brother some money to help them out. I could understand that, but when this excuse started to be used every month and he had zero money to help me pay bills, I started to question his story. It was then that he told me about Charlotte's Internet cafés, which were basically gambling parlors before they were banned. He would go in there and lose his entire check. So not only did I have a convicted felon, I had someone who was addicted to gambling. I talked to him about whether he thought he had a gambling problem, and he got upset at me and insisted that he didn't.

More months passed, and he didn't have the money to help me out with bills and kept lying to me about going to the casino. One day I got off work to see if he was at home like he'd said he was. I got home, and he wasn't there, so I called him. When he answered, I told him I was just calling to let him know that I loved him and wanted to know what he was doing. He told me that he wasn't doing anything, just sitting on the porch. Now I was at home looking out onto an empty porch, so I asked him if he wanted to give the truth another try. He said, "I'm at the casino." The moment those words left his mouth, I hung up the phone. I got in my car to go get him, and even though he told me that he'd won some money, I didn't care. I cussed him out and made him walk home. The fact that he'd continued to gamble, although he had promised me he wouldn't, wasn't the point; it was the fact that he had lied to me about going. If he would lie to me about going to the casino, what else would he lie about? I tried to talk to him again to see if he felt he had a problem. Even if he didn't think he did, could he not see what was going on with our relationship because of his gambling?

We slept in separate rooms for a few days after that blowout. It was one of the darkest arguments we had during our relationship. We finally decided it was time to stop being mad at each other. After that, Ray was being really sweet toward me over the next few weeks, getting me flowers and doing a lot of the cooking. After I forgave him, things started to get back to how they'd been when we first started dating. He would still have his times where he questioned if he wanted to be in a relationship or not, but since that happened so often, I grew to accept it for what it was. I could almost set my calendar to it since it came around the same time every month.

When his mother moved, however, the arguments started to come closer together. I didn't realize how much of a mother's boy he was until his mother wasn't around. Don't get me wrong—I'm a mother's boy as well, but I do not arrange my relationships based on where my mother is located. All I heard from him was how he thought about moving to where she was. I knew I didn't want to move, so I didn't know how things would be if he actually decided to move.

Ray decided to take a trip to visit his friends and his family. To be honest, I needed the time away, but this was the first time we had been apart since we'd gotten together. It was nice not having to really worry about him, but the codependent side of me wanted him to come back and be around me so I could know what he was doing and when. He was only gone for a few days, but it felt like an eternity to me. I came to some harsh realizations when he wasn't around. I realized that I needed him just as much as he needed me. He gave me purpose in our relationship; it motivated me to know that he depended on me. In many ways he enabled my codependent behavior. I couldn't see it while I was in it, but our relationship was not a healthy one. When I finally realized what was going on, however, I didn't care enough about it to want to change it.

When Ray finally came back, he showed me just how much he had missed me, which led to the best sex I'd ever had—with him, anyway. I asked him how he felt about wanting to move after he had the visit, and he told me he still wanted to but just not at the moment. For me, that was good enough to keep me satisfied since that gave me more time to try and convince him to stay.

Being the detective I am, I had to figure out if he wanted to move so badly because of some dude he used to talk to when he was there. He left his phone unlocked one day, and I took a look through it and found out he had been messaging one of his ex-boyfriends. This ex, however, lived in Charlotte. He'd told me about how this dude had used him for sex and how that was all the ex thought he was good for—that he had cheated on Ray and how terrible he was. I flipped out, asking why he was still talking to a dude he claimed had cheated on him and treated him so badly. There was no real response to my questions other than Ray saying he was sorry and that he would block the ex. I made sure that I sat there and watched him block him just to ensure he actually did it.

It was coming up on our usual time when Ray would state that he didn't want to be with me, but this time it was actually the end. I had a real long day at work, and when I got home, I wanted nothing more than love and attention. When I got there, however, I was met with attitude and dryness. I realized that he had a condition, so I asked him what was wrong. He said, "Nothing." He was having one of his spells where he would get all in his feelings. I figured the best thing to do was to leave him be to avoid having an argument. Before I decided to do that, however, I let him know how I'd had a long day, and all he'd done was sit there, and now that I was home, I had to deal with his dry attitude.

I decided to walk to the store to give him some space. When I was on my way back, he called me. He just flat out told me he wasn't happy and that he wanted to dump me and move to be closer to his mother. I told him there was no way in hell that he was just going to dump me over the phone and that I deserved a hell of a lot more than that. I ran all the way back to the apartment and hoped that he was just in his feelings—and that when I actually got back, he would change his mind. I asked him if he was serious, and he looked at me and said, "I just don't want to be with you anymore."

I paused. I thought about all the days I got up to go to work at a job I hated while he sat there watching TV all day, doing nothing. I get that when you're a felon, it is harder for you to find a job, but he wasn't even trying. When he said those words to me, something in me snapped. I couldn't believe the nerve of this bastard. I said to him, "OK, since that's what you want, let me help you out the door." I started grabbing all of his clothes out of the closet and throwing them on the floor; I tossed out all of his shoes, jackets, and hats. I told him to get all of his shit and get the fuck out of my house. He started moving, but he wasn't doing it fast enough for me, so I started yelling. I'm not sure what came over me, but I didn't care. He didn't have a car or a ride since nobody fooled with him like that, so I told him to put his stuff in my car, and I would just take him to his brother's house. Even while being dumped, I was still being the bigger person and helping him out.

One thing I wish we had done was just give each other space for the entire day. Perhaps we would've broken up later, but I don't think we would've broken up in that manner. Once the adrenaline wore off, my emotions took a sudden turn. I was crying and begging him not to do this, saying he just needed some time to himself, but he refused to talk to me. I've begged a guy to not dump me before, but this had to be the worst feeling—pleading and begging a man to stay with me and him being so cold toward me. I think that was the hardest thing for me to deal with—the silence and his refusal to even acknowledge me even though I was the one giving him a ride.

We arrived at his brother's house, and I flat out asked him, "Are you not going to say anything to me?"

He looked at me and said, "I have nothing to say."

I just broke down right there in his brother's driveway as I waited until Ray got all his stuff out of my car.

That drive back to my apartment was so rough… I'd been dumped before, yes, but this one felt so different. I felt like I'd given and given and tried and tried for months to make this relationship work while he practically had a free ride, and I was the one who got dumped. Selfishly I thought about never being able to get that dick again.

I was so angry that I completely cut myself off from everyone for weeks. This was the first time I really thought about killing myself. I felt worthless. I was at the end of my rope with love and giving dudes a try. I really wanted to die. I didn't eat anything for a few days, and when I started to eat, it was only one small thing a day. I didn't want to talk to anyone; I didn't want advice or any "I told you sos." Just like after all the other breakups, I didn't get out of bed, and I barely went to work. This felt like the worst breakup I'd ever had. I'd dated guys for longer than this relationship lasted and hadn't felt that type of pain. No, this was different. The main thing I'd become dependent on was no longer here for me. My heart felt like it had been ripped out of my chest. It took me months to get right after this breakup. I dove into depression and started having all types of sex with random people, I started to drink really heavily, and I just didn't want to be alive anymore. I didn't think that not being with Ray would cause me so much pain, but I guess that's what being in a codependent relationship will do to you.

I really thought he would call me and try to get me back. I mean, his looks and good dick aside, he didn't have anything else going for him, and who would want to put up with that? He called me a few weeks after the breakup, but it wasn't to get me back; it was only to check on me and confirm his decision. I didn't want to hear that, so I just hung up on him. Why call me and further kick me when I was down?

It was suggested to me that I give counseling a try. I'm not sure what the stigma is in the African American community about counseling, but I decided to give it a try to see if it would help me. I found a male counselor I felt comfortable talking to and decided to go see him a few times a month, at least until I got over my depression. I was so low, he informed me that I should get on antidepressants, which I did. I felt so numb for months after that breakup.

I learned a lot about myself from going to counseling. I learned that since I didn't have a steady father figure in my life, I was looking to fill that void with the men I dated. I also picked men I could take care of in a sense, men who made me feel wanted and needed. Taking care of a man made me feel like he wouldn't leave me; it gave me some type of power over who stayed in my life. I was sadly wrong though. I stayed in counseling for months. Some days I felt great, other days not so great, but overall, counseling was the best thing I've ever done for myself, or anyone else for that matter. I had to prepare myself mentally for when I ran into Ray again. I needed to be in a stronger place and not do my usual routine of getting over my last guy by quickly getting under a new guy. I made a promise to God and myself that I would take time to work on me—not be a fool for love anymore—and take a break from sex.

9

DL THUG BOTTOM

I worked on myself for a full year straight. I didn't talk to any dudes, I didn't have sex with anyone, and I managed to pull myself out of the depression I was in and come off my antidepressants. I may not have been ready to start dating again, but it had been too long since I'd gotten some, so I took a look through Jack'd which was a new gay dating app. I wasn't on long before I got messaged from DL Thug Bottom, who didn't have a profile picture. Usually I don't deal with anyone without a photo, but when I asked him for one, he sent me one of his face. I questioned why didn't he show his face by default, and he told me that he was on the down low. "Here we go again," I said, but I wasn't looking for a boyfriend, so it didn't matter to me.

I must admit I was instantly attracted to him, and since he lived right around the corner from me, I

figured I'd give him a chance to spit some game. After
a few messages and a quick call, I decided to pay him
a visit. After the first five minutes, I realized we had
a real connection. I mean any dude that can talk shit
with me is definitely worth my attention. I knew what I
was coming over there for, so we ended up in his bedroom, and before you know it my dick was in his ass. I
usually don't do the unprotected-sex thing, especially
in this lifestyle, but I was feeling adventurous. The sex
was insanely good. This guy definitely wins the gold
for some of the tricks he was able to perform. After we
finished we went back into the living room to watch
TV. I felt pretty comfortable around him; I mean, we'd
just had sex.

We saw each other every day for the next week,
talked all the time on the phone, and texted each other constantly. We spent just about every day with each
other for a month straight. We were moving so fast, but
I didn't care how fast we were moving; I was enjoying
the ride.

Things took a weird turn when Mr. Thug Bottom
told me he loved me. We spent so much time with each
other having incredible sex that I slipped and told him
I loved him too. I wasn't sure if I really did or if I was
just dickmatized, but I just went along with it. Only
thing about him was that we couldn't go anywhere
together: not on a date, not to the movies, not even
to the gas station. He was so afraid of being found
out, our evenings always ended with us just staying in

the house. I've dated down low guys where we at least could go out in public but just couldn't show affection to each other. Fine at first, but eventually that gets old and boring.

I didn't think love would start to separate you from the person you say you have it for, but I guess sometimes it does. DL Thug Bottom started acting funny toward me after he said those three words. I couldn't pinpoint why at first, but I'm not a beat-around-the-bush kinda person, so I asked. Turns out he'd never been in love with a dude before, and the thought of it scared him. All I could do was make him feel that I understood what he was feeling, but when is being in love with someone a thing to be scared of? He refused to tell me he loved me again, even after I said it to him after we had the conversation. He went into total shutdown with me, and I was like, "So you're just going to pretend that you never told me you loved me?"

As time went on, I tried to get closer to him, and he started to pull back, but we really hit a bump in the road when he told me that when he went back home, he still slept with this girl. He said for me not to worry though, because I was the only dude he was sleeping with. As if somehow that made it better for me. My counter for that was, "OK, since you can sleep with women still, I'm going to go do my own thing with any man I want to." I, however, was in the wrong if I did anything with anyone else other than him.

This was the beginning of the end for whatever it was we had going on. What was once enjoyable became petty arguments over my being his dirty little secret. I asked him if he had any intention to stop having sex with her. We weren't dating, but I'd thought we had a mutual respect that we were going to focus on each other while we figured things out. He flat out told me that he had no plans to stop doing what he was doing. I just said OK and continued to sleep with him and let him go do his thing whenever he went home.

Why is it that good dick can make you go crazy? I knew what it was doing to me, but I didn't care. I needed my fix, and he was happy to supply it to me, so I didn't care what toll it was taking on me mentally and physically; I just knew I had to have it. I tried to distance myself from him, but it seemed the more I pulled back, the more I wanted him. It got to the point where we were fucking every day. DL Thug Bottom was one of the best dudes I have slept with. I was addicted to his sex; I couldn't leave him alone. His dick was like crack to me. He was so freaky too and was as good a bottom as he was a top. I knew that I needed more than sex, but I didn't want to cut him off because I would miss it; he had enough need to supply the demand.

One day he came over to watch movies, which usually wound up with us having sex, but something seemed off about him. He smelled different than usual. He was normally fresh and smelled of his cologne, which usually helped me get in the mood. This time he smelled like sex; it was a faint smell, but I knew what it was. The movie was over, and I could tell he wanted to get into the sex part of our evening. He started to undress, and when he removed his underwear, I was hit with the aroma of dick and ass, and it wasn't his. He must've seen my face, because he asked, "What's wrong with you?"

I had to ask him, "You fucked someone else before you came here, didn't you?"

"What? That's crazy—of course I didn't," he replied.

"Then why do you smell like straight sex masked by cologne?"

After I'd asked him the same question a few times, he finally told me the truth: he'd had sex with some random dude he'd met on Jack'd before he came over to my house. Again, we weren't in a relationship, so it's not like he'd cheated on me, but what we did have was mutual respect, and we had decided that we weren't going to be talking to anyone else—besides the girl he got to sleep with when he went home. "How could you just come straight here without even going to wash your ass?" It takes a nasty kind of dude to come straight to your house wanting to have sex without washing off the smell and the juices from his last fuck.

We clearly weren't having sex that night. I told him to pull up his pants and go wash his ass since he had already gotten off. He huffed and cussed, but he got his ass out of my apartment.

I needed a break from him for a while, and I finally convinced him that we needed a break to see if this was something we really wanted to continue to do. It was nice not having to prepare for sex every day, as I was starting to get tired of having it on a constant basis. My body was tired and needed to rest.

A few weeks passed, and we reconnected. We were back on our fairy-tale romance, and things seemed to have leveled off...until I sent him a text asking him to go out with me. I'd had enough of being inside with this guy. It had been months, and DL Thug Bottom and I hadn't done anything together outside of our homes. Who knew that asking someone out to the movies would cause such a huge argument? But that is exactly what happened. He told me that he wasn't ready for the public eye yet and that I could take it how I wanted, but the answer was no. Back in the days when I used to have signatures for each text message I sent out, I had "chapter II" as my signature to signify my new start on my life, and that only added fuel to this argument as he took that as a personal attack on him. He claimed I was waving my "chapter II" shit in his face and said he wasn't going out with me, and nothing I could say would change his mind.

I remember saying to myself, "It's decision time. Do you want to continue dealing with someone who will never take you out in public and will continue to do his thing with women while he is with you? Or will you stand up for yourself and walk away from the situation?" I finally decided enough was enough. The argument that had started because I wanted to go to the movies showed me what kind of person he was. The dick-covered veil was finally lifted, and I was seeing clearly.

Funny how when you argue with someone, all the pettiness of a person shows. He decided his last words to me would be that every time he was fucking me, he took the condom off when I wasn't paying attention. Apparently this is called "stealthing," which I hadn't realized was a thing, but he allegedly did it on a lot of occasions. It took everything in me not to drive over to his house and kick his teeth down his throat. I felt violated. It's one thing for us to make the decision together to play Russian roulette with our lives, but when you take the decision from me and do what you want, especially since I wasn't the only person you were sleeping with and that opened me up to all kinds of STDs, I have a real problem with that. The worst part about all of this, and all of it was bad, was that when he was telling me that he had been removing the condom during the majority of our sex, he was smiling the entire time. He was even chuckling at parts of the conversation, like there was something fun or funny about having sex with someone and taking off the condom without his knowledge or consent. I really wanted to knock that smug look off his face, but what would that do? If anything, it would probably give him even more satisfaction for what he'd done, so instead my last words to this fool before I blocked his ass were, "I wish you nothing but the best."

10

PEPPER SPRAY AND LOVE THAT'S HERE TO STAY

After the news Mr. Thug Bottom gave me, I had to take another break from sex and go get tested for everything under the sun to make sure I hadn't caught anything from him. Everything came back clean, but I decided to take a break from bottoming for guys. I was still having a lot of oral and topping other dudes, but I didn't want to have another guy top me until I got into a serious relationship.

In October 2013, in another fit of horniness, I went on my favorite hookup app, jokingly of course, Jack'd. I saw this cute guy, Demetrius, and decided to message him, but I was on a mission to get some head, some ass, or both. He agreed to get a little kinky and came right on over. I had to shower and prep for his arrival. After about thirty minutes, he knocked on my door, and when I let him in, the first thing I noticed was his ass. I'm more of a bottom, but I can appreciate a nice ass when I see it. We got right down to what I wanted, which was getting some head, and boy, did he know how to do it. After I got off, he took off. It was nice being able to have my need satisfied and let that be that.

We didn't talk too much afterward other than small talk here and there. I was feeling horny again, but this time I wanted some ass. I remembered how nice Demetrius's ass was and figured I would hit him up to see if he was interested. He obliged and came right over. He was looking good and had on some pants that showed off his ass. Again we got right down to business. The sex was incredible, and it was nice being able to flex my top muscles. After we'd had sex, he took off, but this time we started communicating a lot more. What started off as sex slowly became infatuation.

Demetrius was wanting some help with his résumé, and since I had some experience with working on résumés, I offered to help him out. Again, I invited him over to the house. This time it wasn't about sex, which was nice; we hadn't had much time to sit and talk. I asked him if he wanted to ride with me to the store after I helped with his résumé. On the way to the store, he held my hand in the car, which I thought was sweet. I felt so comfortable around him. It was a nice change of pace compared to what I'd had with other guys. We arrived back at my apartment, and he had to go. As he was walking out, he pulled me close to him, and we kissed. This wasn't any ordinary kiss; this was nothing but pure passion. Not sexual, just passion. He told me to give him a call later, and he left. I must admit, I was feeling butterflies for the rest of the night. It was one of the more enjoyable times I've had with a guy without taking my pants off.

I was heading home to South Carolina that weekend, so I knew I wouldn't see him for a few days, which was fine since we didn't have any type of commitment yet. The weekend had arrived, and I headed home. We stayed up all night texting and talking while I was home. We had such an amazing conversation that it was the first day I started to catch real feelings for him.

A few months passed, and surprisingly the communication remained steady. I was used to not having a steady flow of conversations from a guy, especially for so long. Demetrius had this ex he was living with that he said was on the crazy side, but I knew how to handle people like that, so I wasn't very worried. I decided to ask if he wanted to spend the night with me one weekend so we could talk. It was nice being around someone and feeling I could be myself without putting on a faker side of me.

Since we were getting serious, I thought it would be a good idea to refrain from sex until we established a serious relationship, even though he had already gotten my dick but not my ass. It's one thing to have sex with someone when there aren't any emotions behind it, but once emotions get involved, sex can complicate things quickly.

I usually get flowers, I don't give them, but I wanted to surprise him with some when he came over later that day since he was having a rough day at work. He loved the flowers, and we had a great night filled with laughing and talking.

Life went on with Demetrius drama free for another month—that is, until I asked him to come over again, and his ex wasn't having it. His ex was getting jealous of how close we were getting and decided to hide his car keys from him because he didn't want Demetrius coming over. I didn't want him to get into it with his ex, so I decided to go over and be a mediator just in case the ex tried to pop off. I didn't come empty handed though: I brought along some pepper spray just in case. I actually grabbed my blade first, but then I thought that would be a bit much.

When I got there, I was instantly hit with "Who the hell are you, and why are you in my house?"

"I'm not here for you, so don't worry about it," I replied.

Demetrius's ex was a little skinny thing that reminded me of an overgrown chihuahua. "Who the hell are you talking to?" he asked.

I could already tell what road this was starting to go down, so I told Demetrius to just pack his stuff; he didn't have to stay there in that toxic environment. I know we hadn't been talking but for a few months, but I could tell he was a really nice guy and just needed out of that situation.

His ex kept popping off and getting into my face, and I kept telling him, "Get the fuck out of my face, dude," but it seemed he just wanted to fight me, and nothing I said was going to make him back off. I gave him one final warning to stay out of my face, and when he came up to me again, I pepper sprayed him in the face. I'd never actually pepper sprayed anyone before, but it was actually kinda fun. My only regret is that I didn't empty the bottle in his retinas. He started screaming and running around the apartment yelling for Demetrius to help him. I gave Demetrius an "I wish you would help him" look.

I decided to walk outside since the smell was so strong, but out came the ex, knocking on neighbors' doors for help. Next thing I know, he took a swing at me, and as I moved out of the way, I tripped and fell. When I got up, we started fighting. I usually keep a clear head, but when you take a swing at me, all of that goes out the window. I had him down on the ground, and I was kicking his head against the concrete. Demetrius pulled me off him, and I almost turned to take a swing at him also. When I'm in the zone, I can't tell whom I'm fighting; I'm just fighting.

You would think getting your ass kicked would humble you, but not this jackass. We all went back inside, and as I was trying to help Demetrius get his stuff so we could just be done and leave, in walked the ex, saying, "I loved this little fight we had—it was cute. I see you had to use pepper spray." I replied that I didn't have to use anything, I was trying not to whoop his ass, and that pepper spray was a courtesy, but since he'd taken a swing, I had to let him know what was up. He started throwing shade about the flowers I'd gotten Demetrius, saying that they looked cheap. To avoid whooping his ass for a second time, I just let him say whatever he wanted to say.

Eventually we got everything loaded and left, headed back to my apartment. I could tell Demetrius was upset. He tried not to show it, but the moment we got back to my apartment and got everything unloaded, he burst into tears. That just made me want to go back and kick his ex's ass all over again. Demetrius is such a sweet guy who seems to only want to be nice and help people, and anyone that hurts people like that really bothers me.

We decided to go to sleep. We'd had a long day and were both really emotional, so sleep was the best thing at this point.

The next morning, we decided it would be a good idea to determine how the bills would be split up. Even though we weren't dating, we still slept in the same bed and did things that couples do. It was weird living with someone I wasn't dating. We had feelings for each other, but we didn't want our current situation to rush along our developing relationship. Demetrius's move in with me was supposed to be only temporary, but the longer he stayed with me, the more I didn't want him to move out. Once the dust settled from fighting that bitch of an ex, we decided to shift the focus to building the strong foundation we wanted our relationship to be based on.

Valentine's Day was approaching, and it was the perfect time for me to see how romantic he could be. He did not disappoint, that was for sure. He cooked for me and got me a few gifts, but most importantly, he made me feel special. I was never too big on Valentine's Day because most of the guys I was with were pieces of shit who didn't want to acknowledge that day at all. Being with a man who wanted to show me how special I was made me feel good. Only thing I was expecting was for him to make it official that we were dating. That didn't happen until a few weeks later, and I must admit I was expecting it on Valentine's Day, so I was a little disappointed when it didn't happen that night, but I knew I couldn't always make things happen when I wanted them to. When he finally did ask me to be his in February 2014, I wasn't expecting a ring to go with it. It wasn't an engagement ring but a promise ring; with that ring he promised to always love me and treat me with the respect that I deserved. When he asked me to be his, I cried. The ring was beautiful, and since I wasn't expecting it, that made it all the more special for me. The gesture behind the ring was so nice; it wasn't something he had to do, but it was that extra mile he went to make me feel special.

This was the first time I was with a man where we didn't argue. Perhaps this was because we took so many months building up our friendship and laying the foundation for a good relationship. After all, they always say best friends make the best relationships.

The hardest part in my relationship with Demetrius was to tell him about my past. I think that is the hardest part of any relationship: talking about the baggage carried from past relationships. I had to give him a lot of the damaging things about me, but like a real man, he didn't turn and run; he wanted to be there for me and help me work through it. To me this was another thing that made Demetrius different. Even though what I had been through was in the past, he still wanted to be there for me and help me get through the pain I was feeling.

As time went on in our relationship, we grew closer as friends and as a couple. It was so weird being with a man out of love and not out of fear of being alone. This was the first time I felt I was truly with someone because I loved him and not for selfish reasons of not wanting to be single—or not wanting anyone else to have him because he was so attractive or his dick game was good. Surprising to me, we made it through our first year without any major incidents…well, unless you call kicking his ex's ass an incident. By this time my entire family had met him, and I had met his family. What was also nice was that everyone on his side liked me, and my family liked him—another first for me, since my family usually ended up hating everyone that I'd ever dated.

As much as I loved living in Charlotte, I had aspirations of making more money. I decided to start looking for jobs in other states; I got lucky and found a job in Newark, Delaware, that was paying six figures. I didn't think I would seriously get the job. I was shocked when I got a phone call back for an interview. After a couple interviews, they extended me the job offer, which I accepted. But I was faced with a dilemma with my relationship. Demetrius and I hadn't been dating long, and when I talked to him about moving to Delaware to pursue this position, I didn't think he would be on board. After we spoke about it, he was in full support of us moving to help further my career. Things were falling into place for me; I finally had a man who was supportive of me, and I had a job paying me six figures before I was thirty. This was the quickest move either of us had ever had to do. We packed up and moved to New Castle, Delaware, two weeks after I had accepted the position. It took us an entire month to be able to move into a house since we'd used all of our money moving. We were crammed into an extended stay during the first month of my employment, but we were finally able to move into our home in September 2014.

The years seemed to pass by so easily with Demetrius. We hardly ever argued, we made each other happy, and we supported each other as a couple should. I was still holding out for my ring when our second year had passed, but again I didn't receive it on any of the dates that I thought I would. As we entered our third year, however, I started to wonder what direction our relationship was heading in. Everything was great as far as our day-to-day things, but I wondered if we were just going to shack up for the rest of our lives. I didn't want to push the marriage issue on him, but I needed to know if it was even going to be on the table. I didn't want to continue living as just Demetrius's boyfriend when in my eyes he was the man I wanted to marry. I didn't know how to have the conversation, but I knew it was something that needed to be had. I was at an impasse: either we planned for our future or maybe it was time to decide if we needed to take a big step back. I decided to plan to have the talk with him when we took our annual trip to Tennessee; this time we decided to take it for his birthday instead of just making it an impromptu trip.

I was glad to be going out of town. I needed a break from reality for a while, and with that conversation looming over my head, I just wanted to get away from Delaware for a while. I didn't want to bring Demetrius down though or cause an argument on his actual birthday, so I decided to hold off on that conversation till the next day.

The next morning came, and we decided to get up early and get a start on the day. He wanted to go to Gatlinburg and spend the day, which was OK with me since there are a lot of places to shop. We took a detour heading there though, stopping at the overlook that looks out on Gatlinburg; it's a big tourist spot. When we got out of the car, he looked so nervous. We started walking toward the cliff, and he asked me, "You know that I love you, right?"

I responded with, "Yes, of course I do," but he just kept repeating that, and all I could think of was, "Did he bring me to this public place to tell me some bad news so I wouldn't make a scene?" Old habits die hard, and something negative was the first thing that popped in my mind.

However, I was so wrong, because he pulled out a ring and got down on his knee and asked me to marry him. He was so nervous he was trembling, and I couldn't do anything but cry. All I could think about was the conversation I wanted to have, and here he was planning to propose to me. "YES!" I yelled. "Of course I'll marry you." He put the ring on my finger and picked me up. Some people were there, and they started yelling congratulations. I was still crying and in complete disbelief over what had just happened. Two years after we'd met, we were finally engaged. All I could do was hug and kiss him. Words can't begin to describe the emotions I was feeling in that moment. Finally, I, Galen, was going to be someone's husband. And what a beautiful place to propose: the weather was perfect, the view was gorgeous, and I was surprised at the amount of support we got from people who were there doing their own thing.

After the big proposal, we went to have a drink to celebrate. All I wanted to do was latch onto him like a tick. I was floating on cloud nine the rest of the trip. The only thing I could think about was the conversation I'd wanted to have with him. Here he had been planning the perfect way to propose to me, and all I'd been thinking about was the way to ask him which direction our relationship was heading. I guess it's true when people say that you can't make things happen when you want them to, because I was blindsided by this proposal. There was no need to have the conversation about the direction of our relationship, as he made it clear to me how he felt the moment he got down on his knee.

I honestly don't remember anything else from this trip. I was so happy to be engaged that everything else paled in comparison to that moment.

I got to plan a wedding like I'd always wanted to, but I wasn't prepared for the level of stress that was involved with that. I enjoyed all the duties and responsibilities of planning our wedding, as I had been planning it in my head for years. It was the most joyful, but at the same time the most stressful, thing I've ever had to do. It seemed that everything that people on Facebook told me could happen, happened. People didn't show up on time to do things, and people who swore they were coming to the wedding didn't show up at all. I wouldn't trade any of it, however, because those are memories that I will cherish and never forget. Times have really changed. Now you can actually go into a store and find Mr. and Mr. wedding items.

The most fun parts were the little times Demetrius and I went to buy things to decorate the wedding with. We laughed, we cried together, we argued over dumb things that didn't matter, and somehow we managed to make it down the aisle anyway.

It took a lot of work to get to this point, not just in my relationship but also on myself. I was a broken man when I met Demetrius, and somehow, I came out on the other side a much better person than when I started. I wouldn't have been able to do that without my husband.

Our wedding day was the most magical day of my life. It seemed to make all of the pain and hurt that I'd been through finally mean something. I married my best friend, the love of my life, on November 4, 2016. I felt that I finally mattered to someone; someone loved me enough to want to spend the rest of his life with me. Most importantly, I didn't have to hurt anymore. I was his husband, and he was mine. I finally had my fairy tale, and I could let go of the past.

So, to my loving husband, Demetrius, thank you for being my rock over the past four years. Words will never describe to you how much I love you and how much you have changed my life.

The End

ABOUT THE AUTHOR

Galen J Cromartie is a wireless software engineer who lives in Charlotte, North Carolina. He was born and raised in Anderson, South Carolina and is a graduate of Tri-County Technical College with an associate's degree in office system technology. He is also a graduate of Lander University with a bachelor's degree in political science. Galen has a love for bowties, computers, mobile devices, and video games. He is also a survivor of domestic violence and was asked to participate in the Emerge Philly October 2017 campaign sponsored by the Choose Courage Foundation that celebrated six survivors of domestic violence. He is the first African American male to be photographed by the Choose Courage Foundation. He is genuinely a shy person, although his writing style can be very bold and out-spoken. He is a video game enthusiast with a love for Mortal Kombat. Galen and his husband enjoys spending their spare time watching horror movies and getting on each other's nerves. Galen has a real interest in hearing other domestic violence survivor's stories and he hopes to continue raising awareness for domestic violence.

GalenJC.squarespace.com
Facebook.com/GalenJCromartie
Instagram: @thebowtiegenuis

Made in the USA
Columbia, SC
16 April 2024